THE ART OF MANDALA COLORING BOOK

Volume 1

By Alessandro Zamboni

WELCOME TO THE ART OF MANDALA!

I'm so happy you decided to purchase my first book of a long series about mandalas, the ancient Tibetan art of drawing these beautiful geometric figures with the sand.

This time we don't have sand, but just paper! And you can photocopy each one of the 50 mandalas as many times as you like to color them as you like. Coloring mandalas give calm, relaxation, happiness and keep stress away.

Mandalas are great for children, awesome for adults and special for elderly people. They were experimented in many situations, and they always came out as winners.

Be ready to get out your pencils, markers, crayons, oil colors and whatever you like to paint with, and be ready to color your series of mandalas, as a hobby, as a relax, or just for pleasure alone or with friends and family members! You are at the center of the mandala universe now!

Thanks so much and have a wonderful travel in the ancient world of mandalas!

Alessandro Zamboni

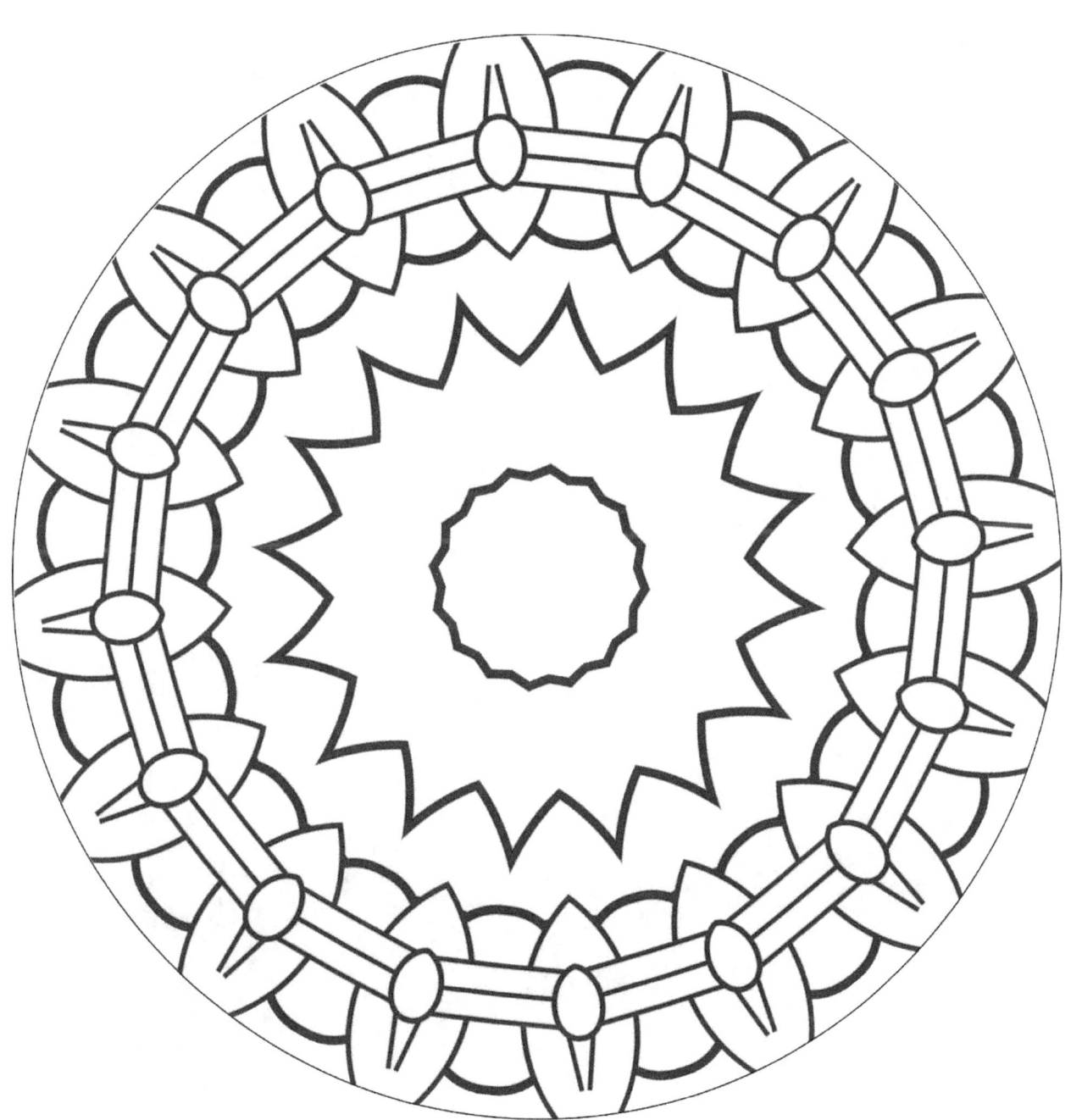

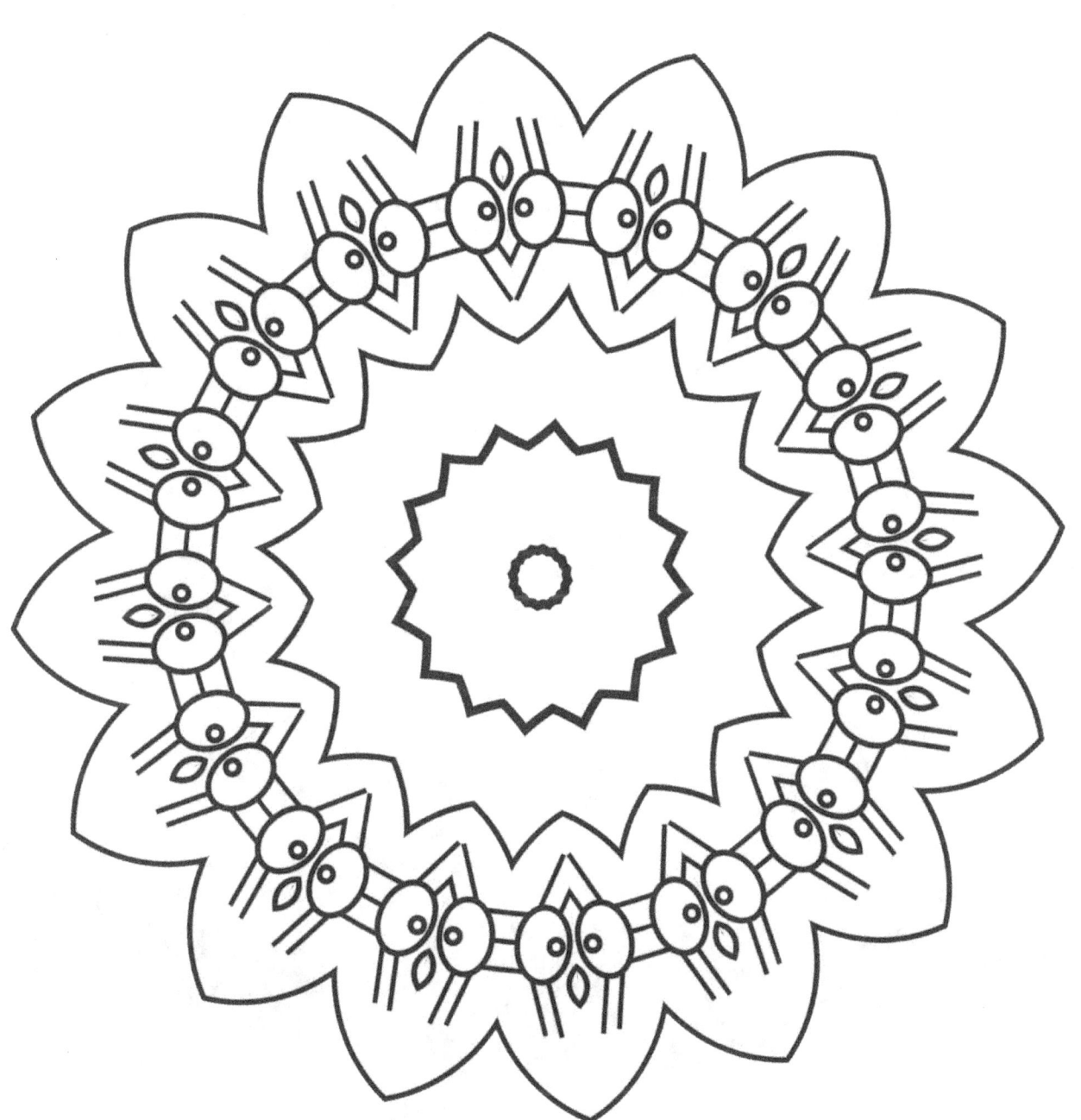

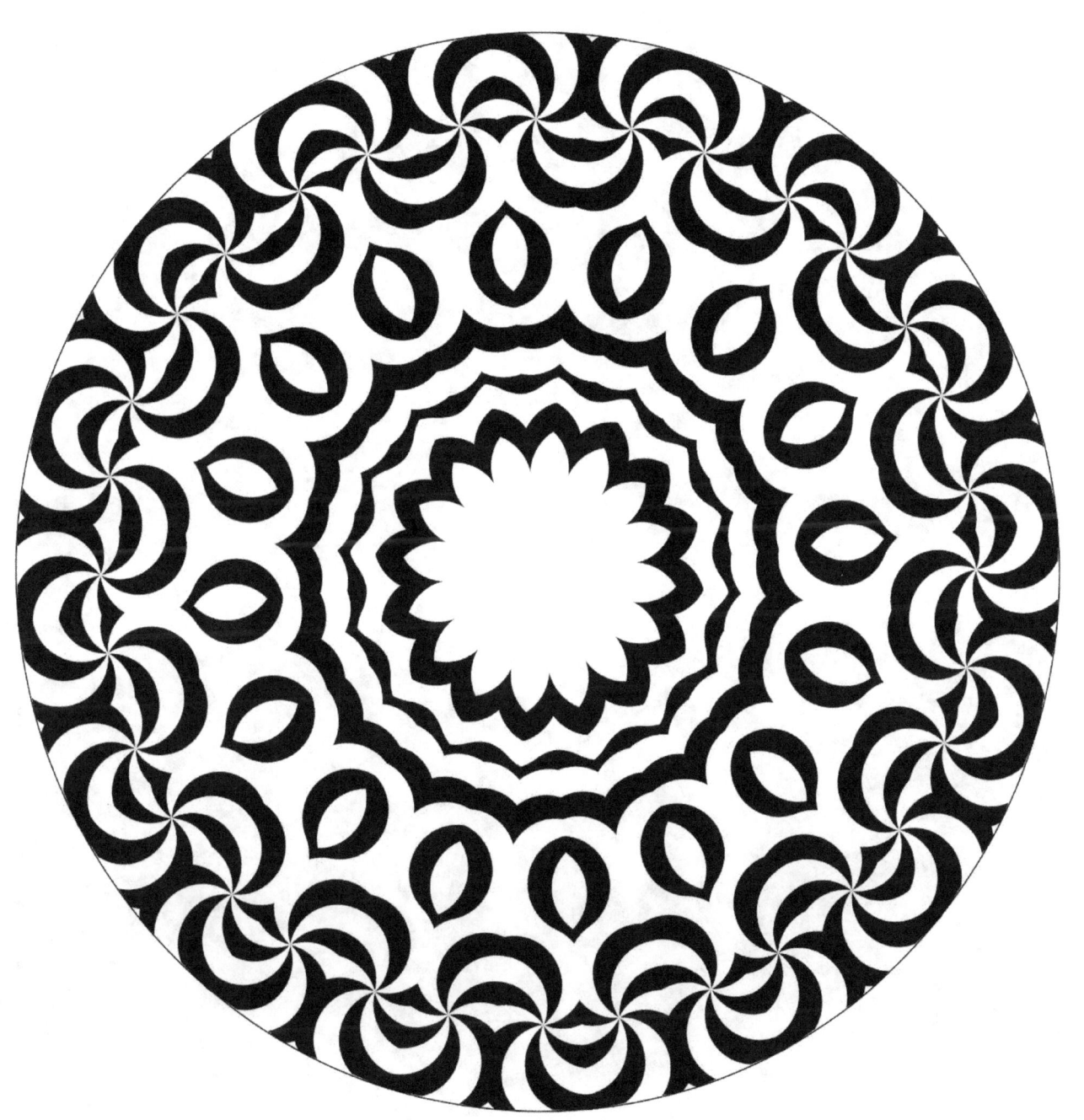

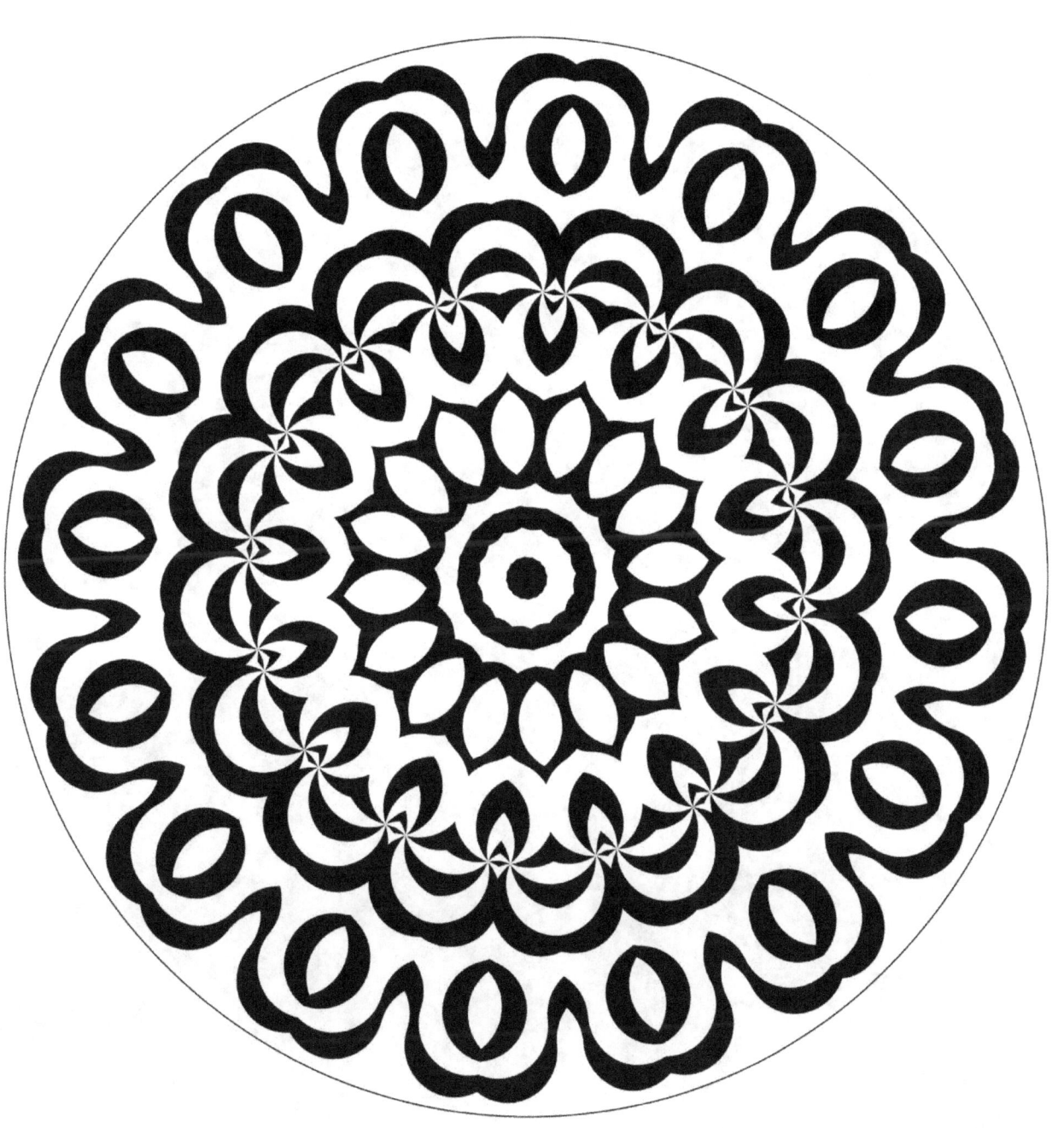

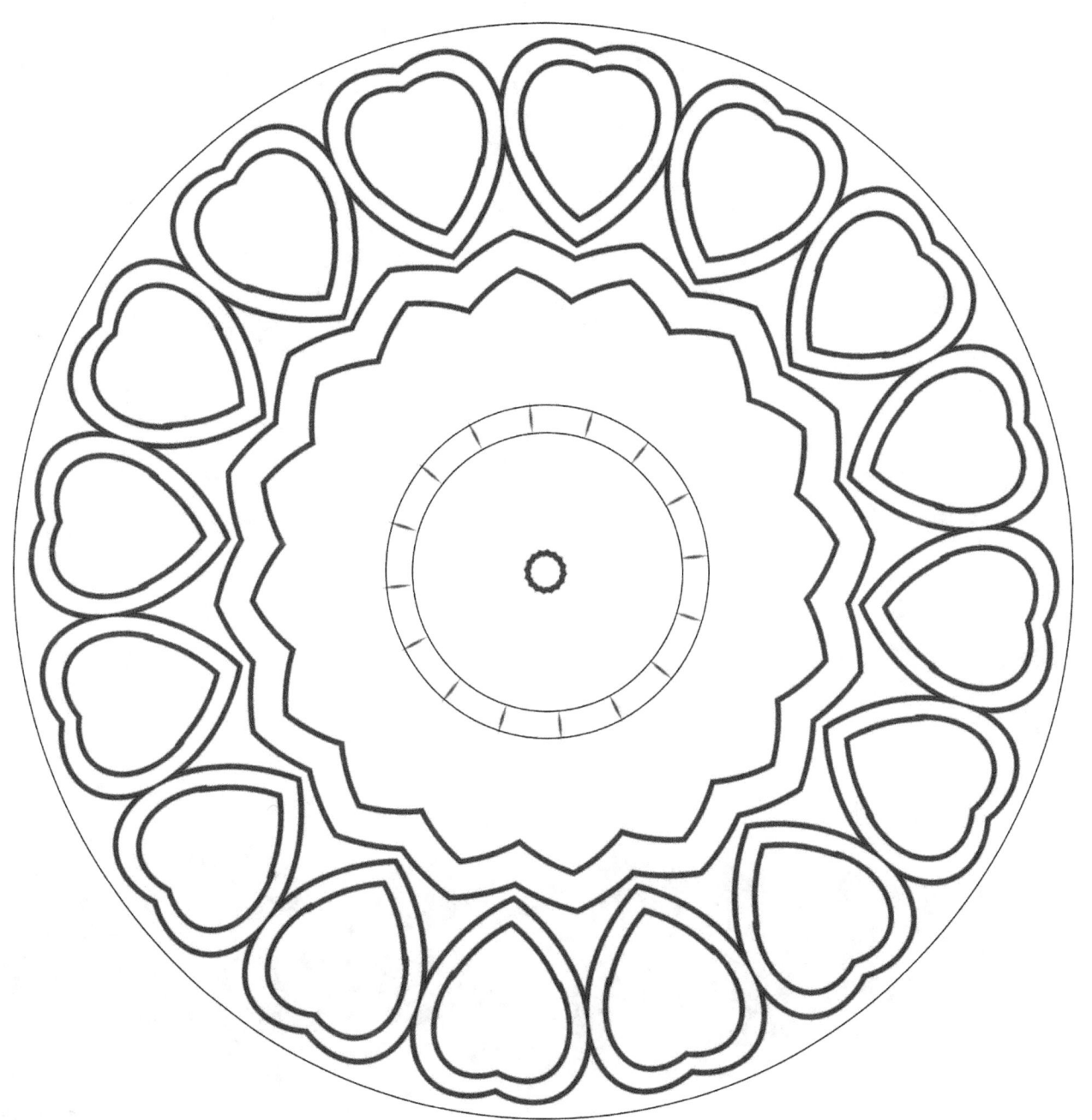

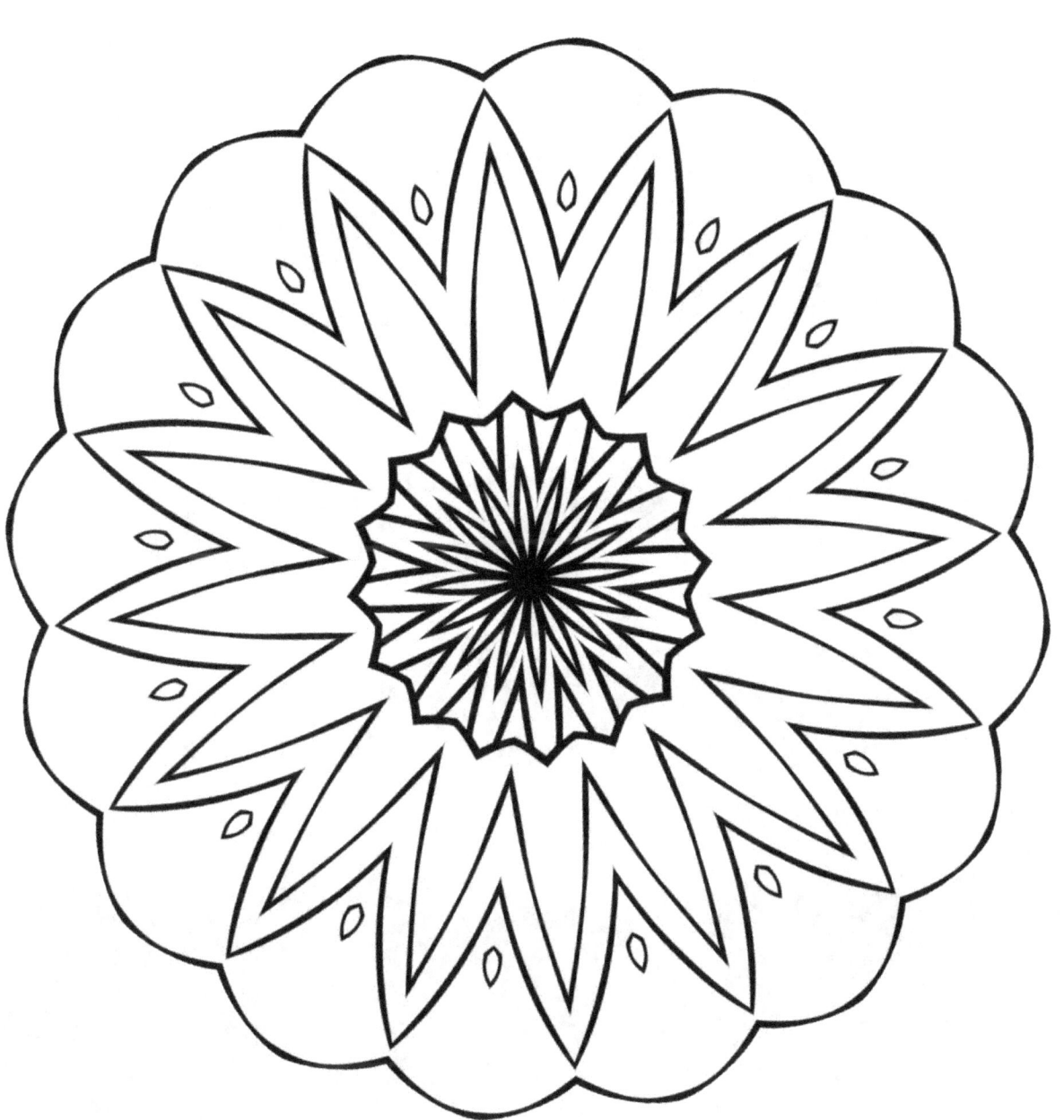

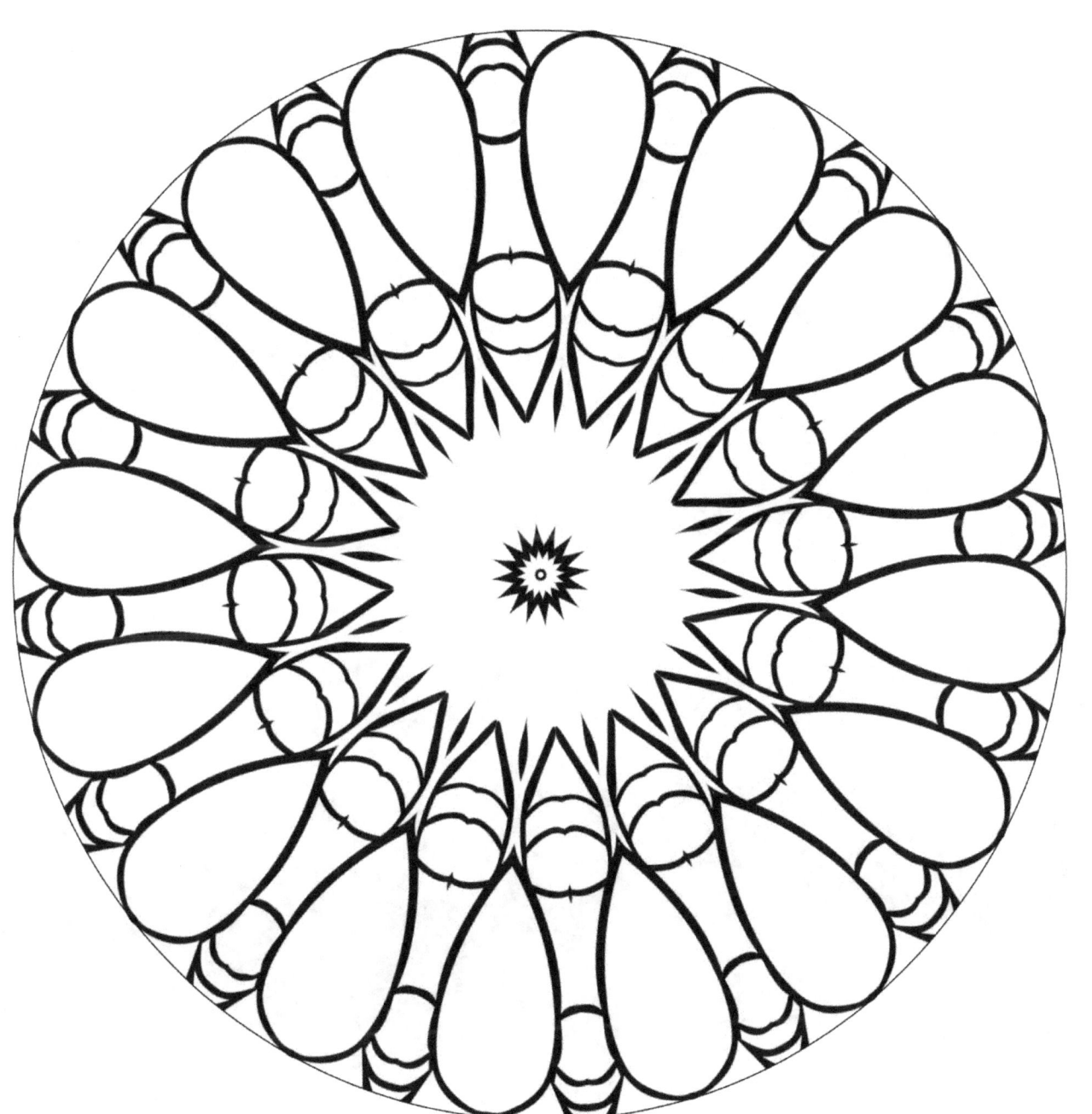

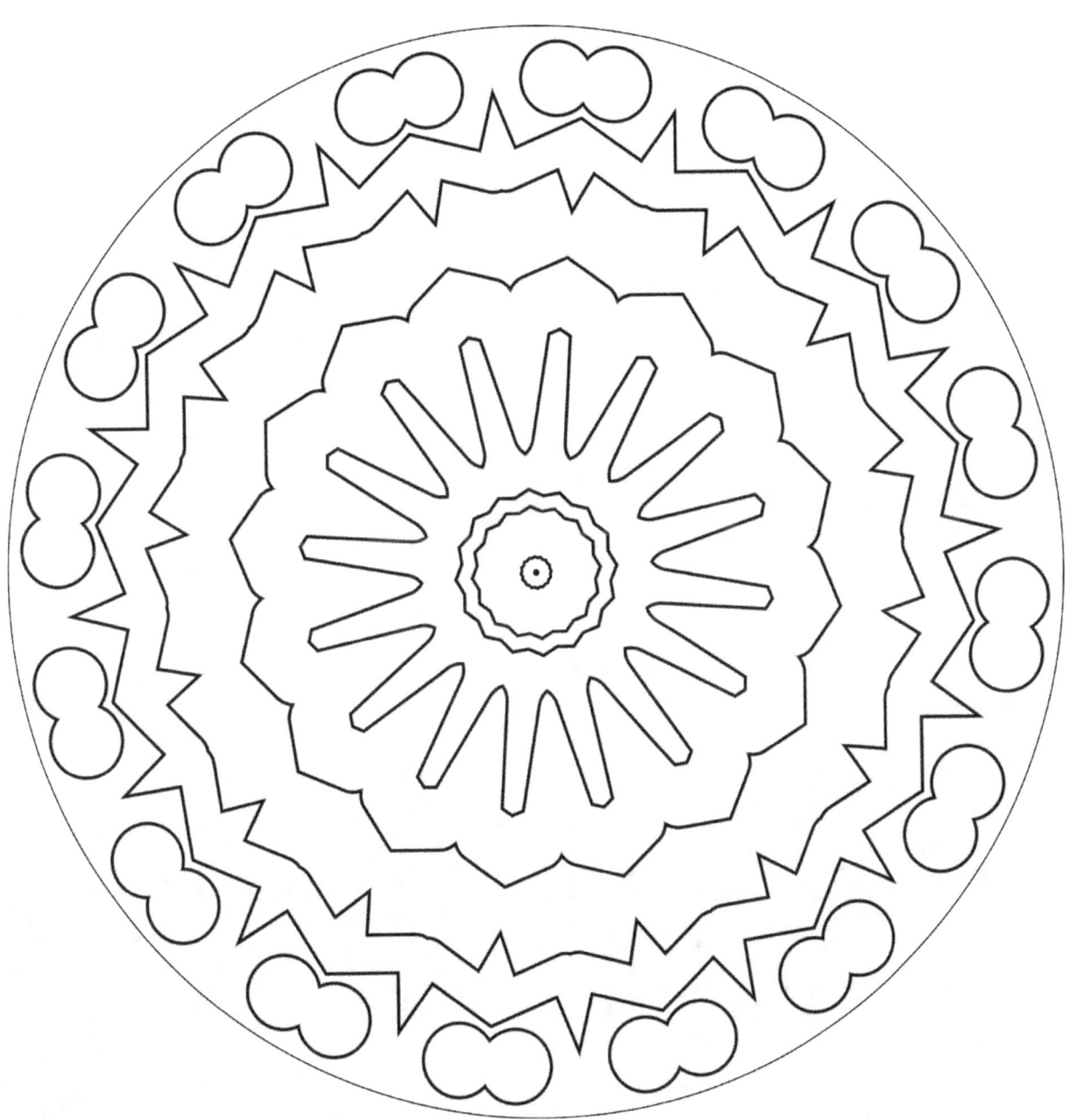

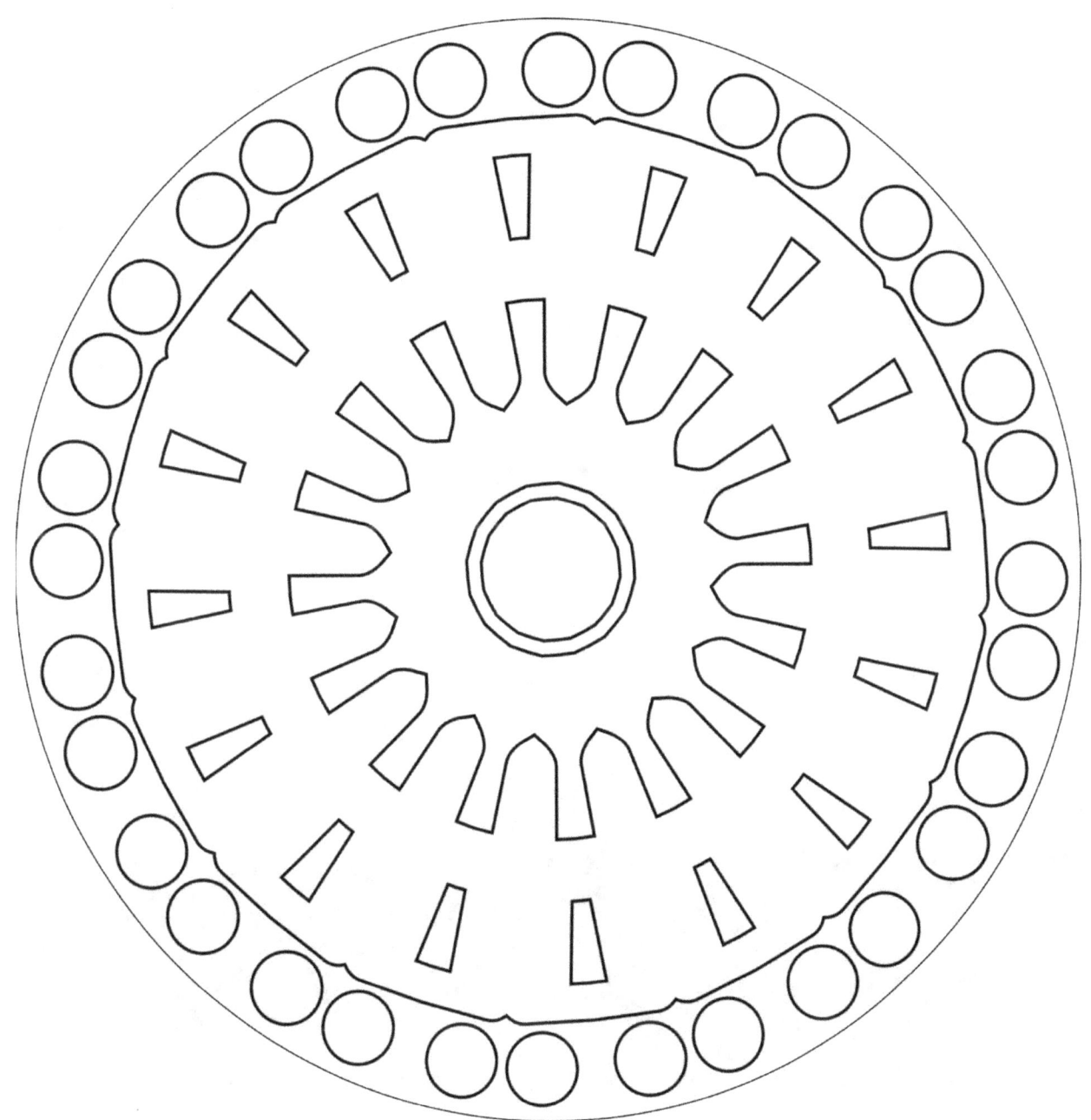

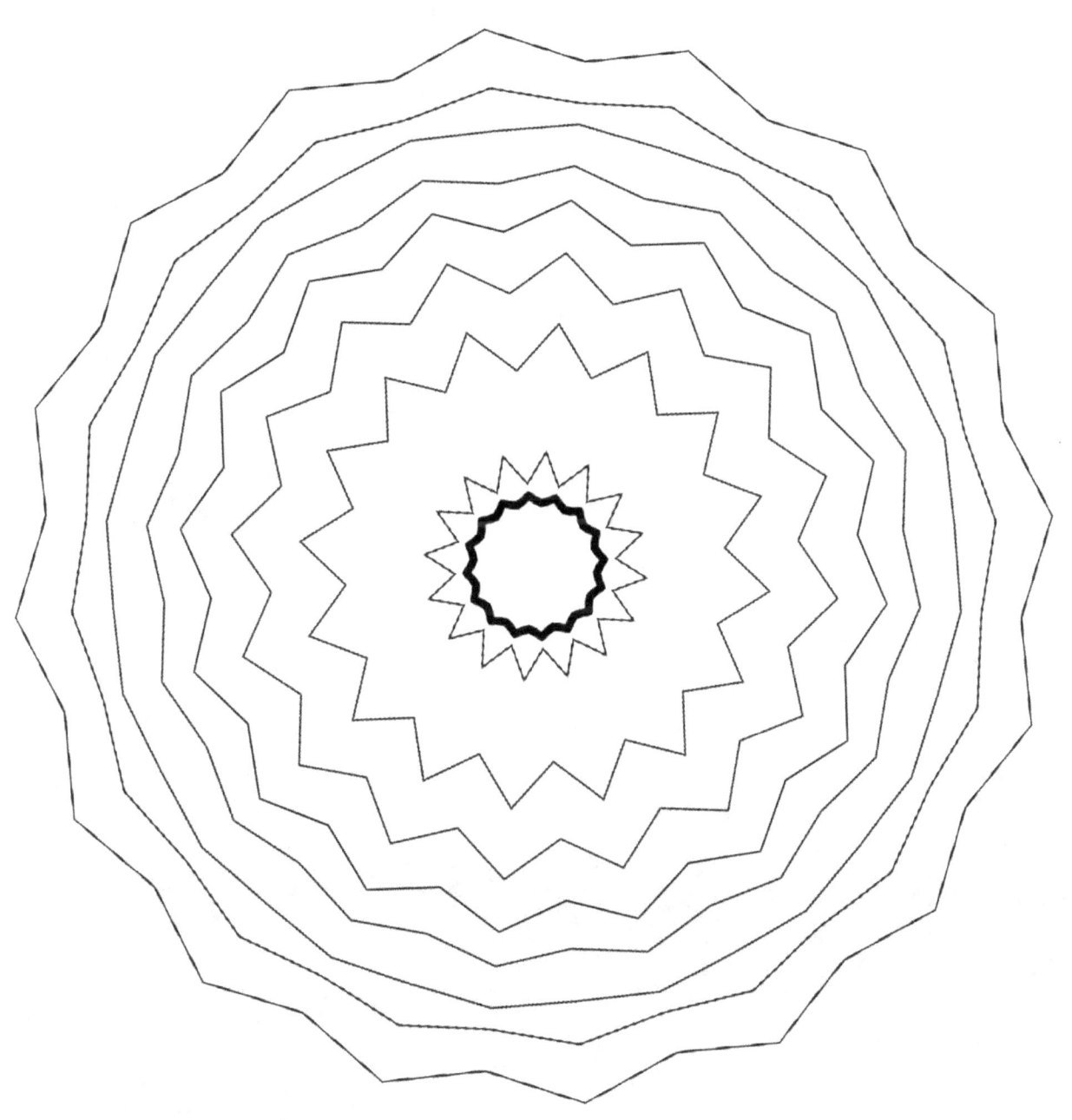

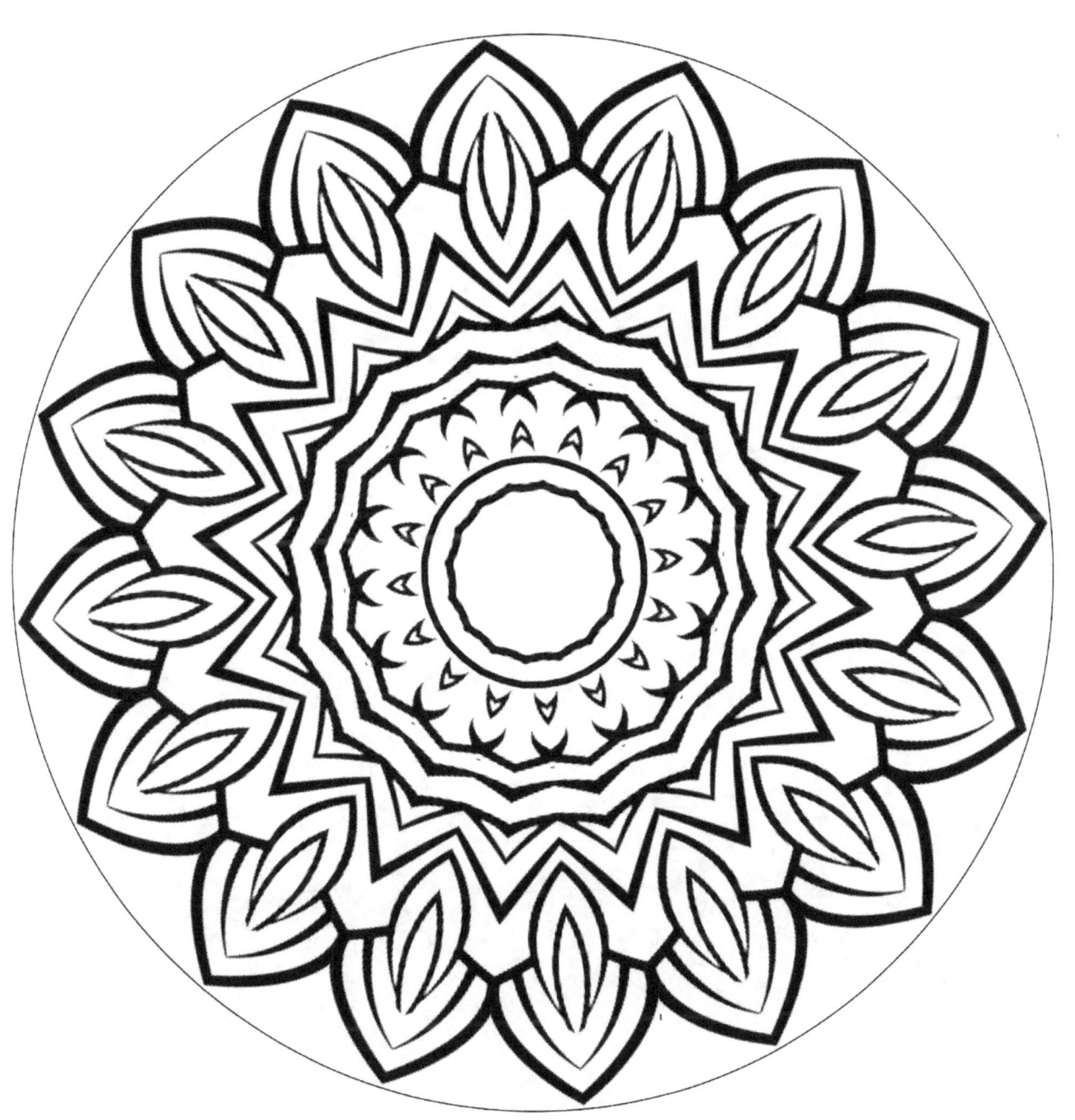

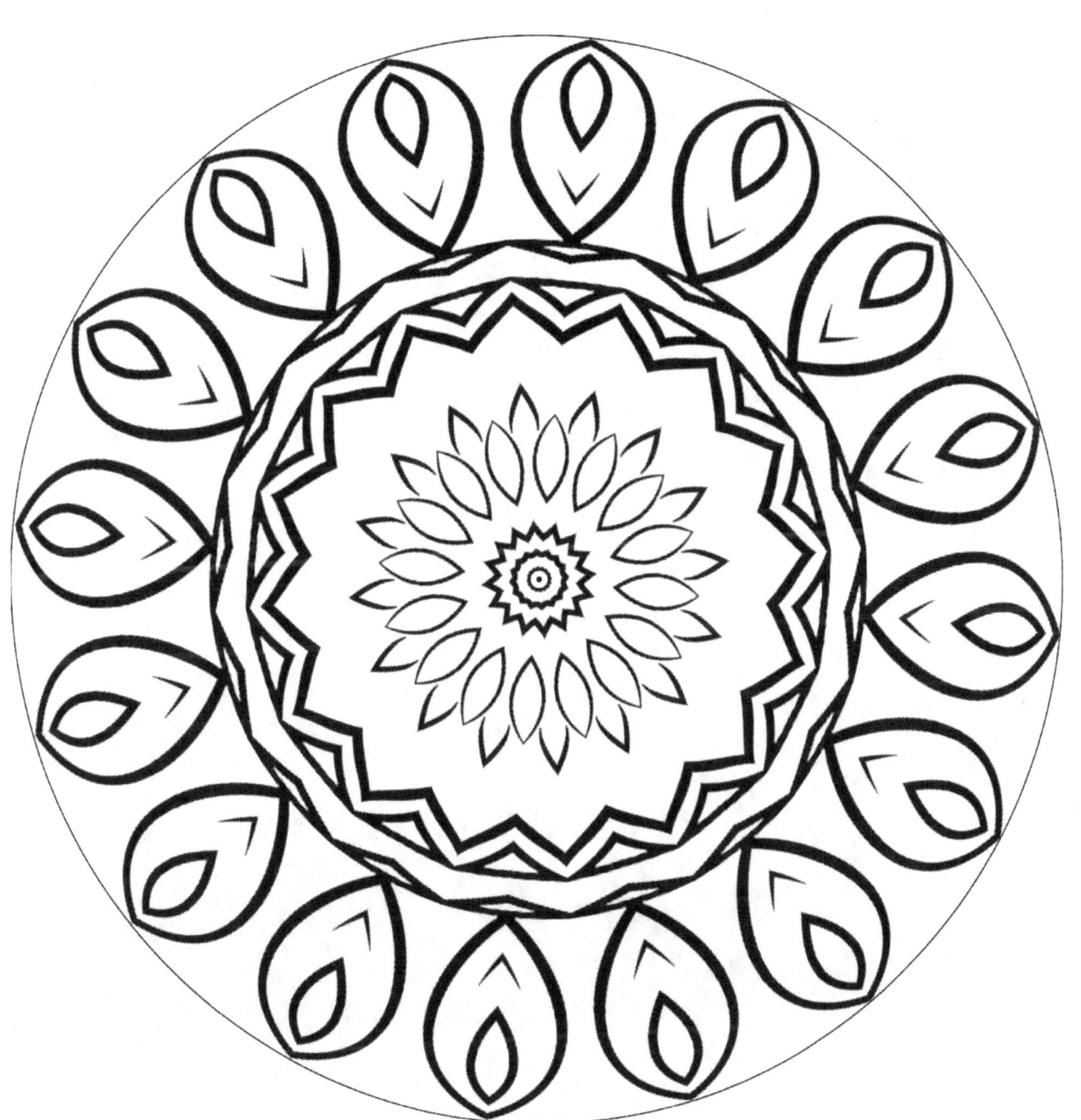

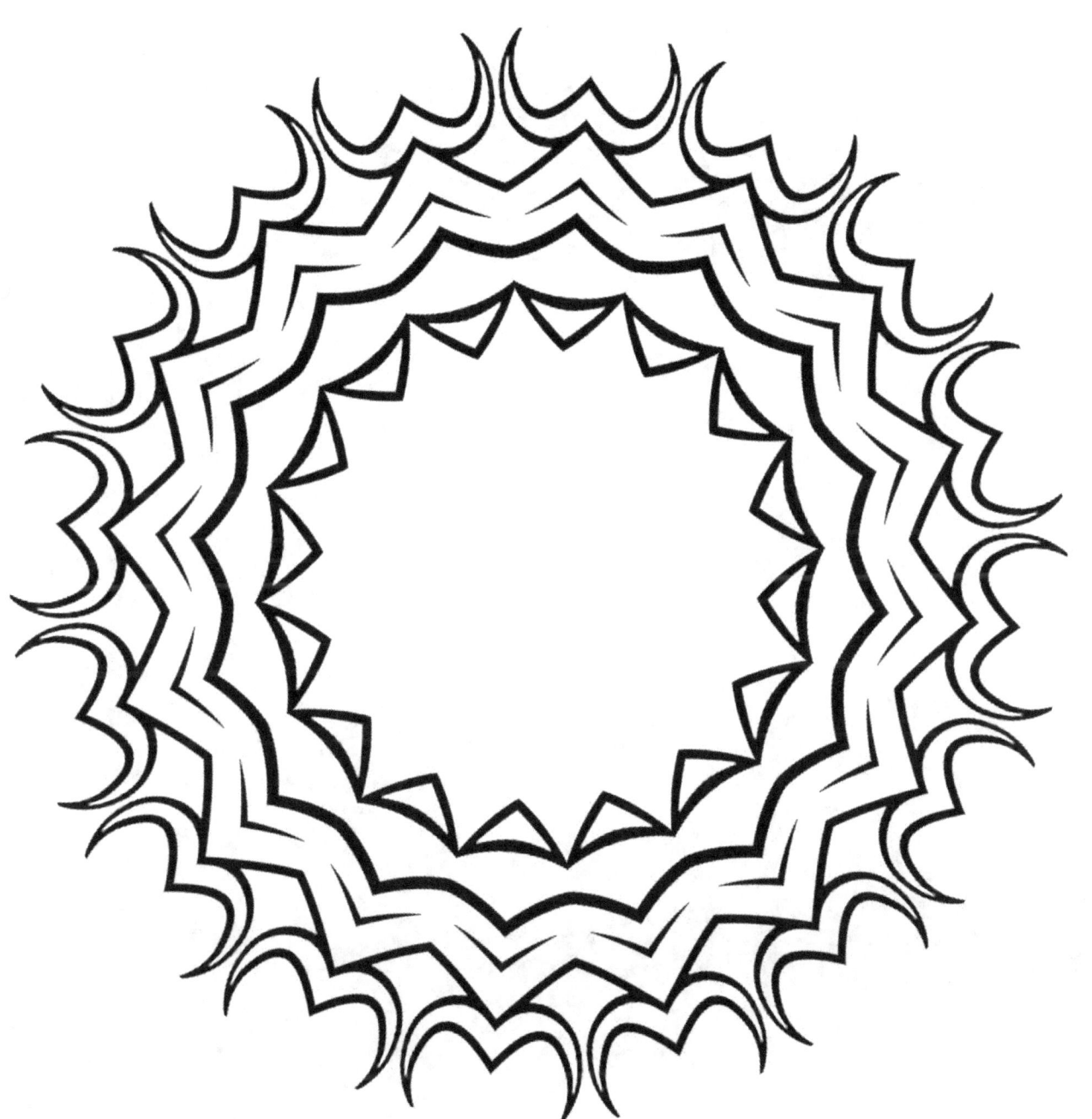

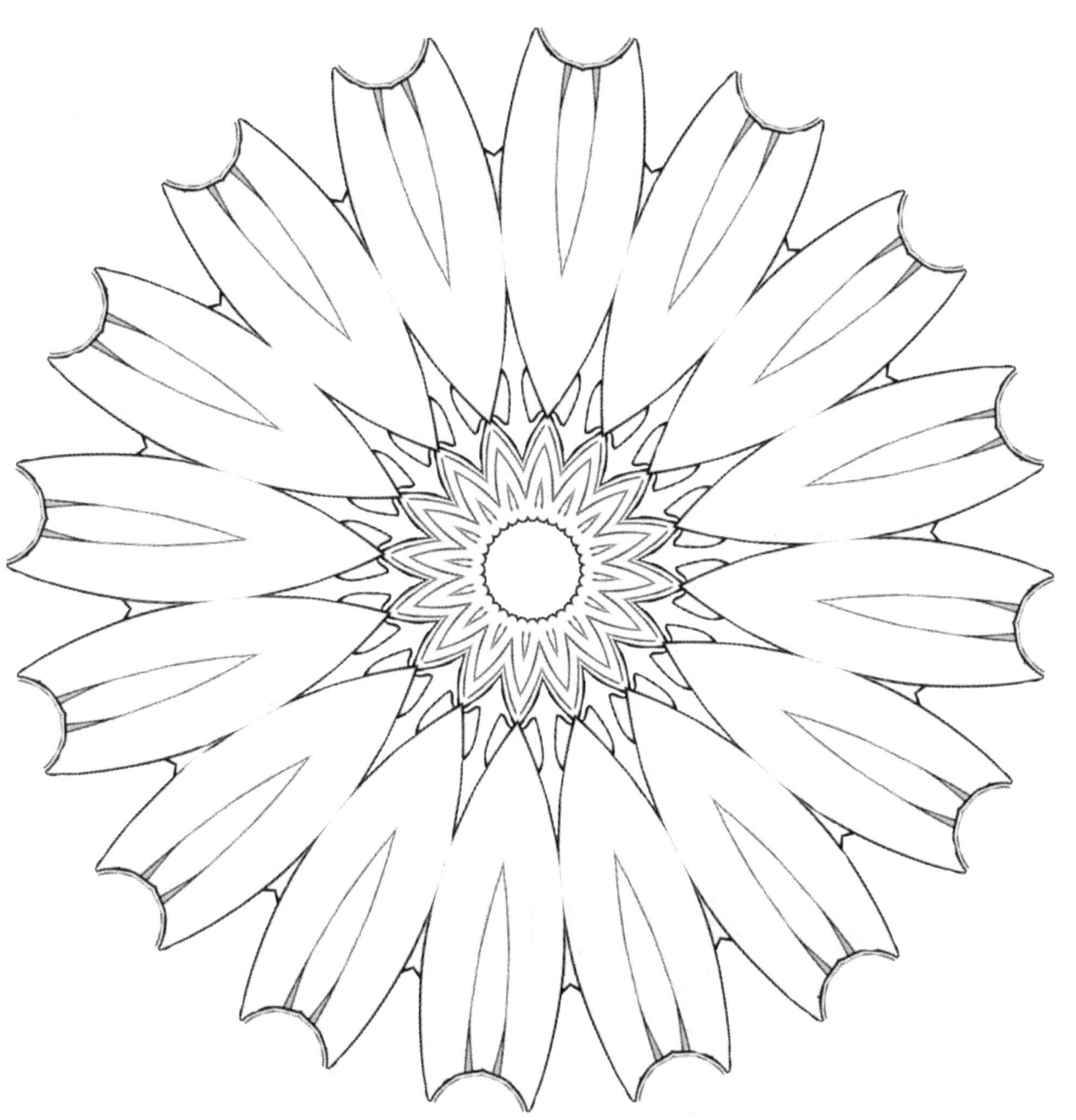

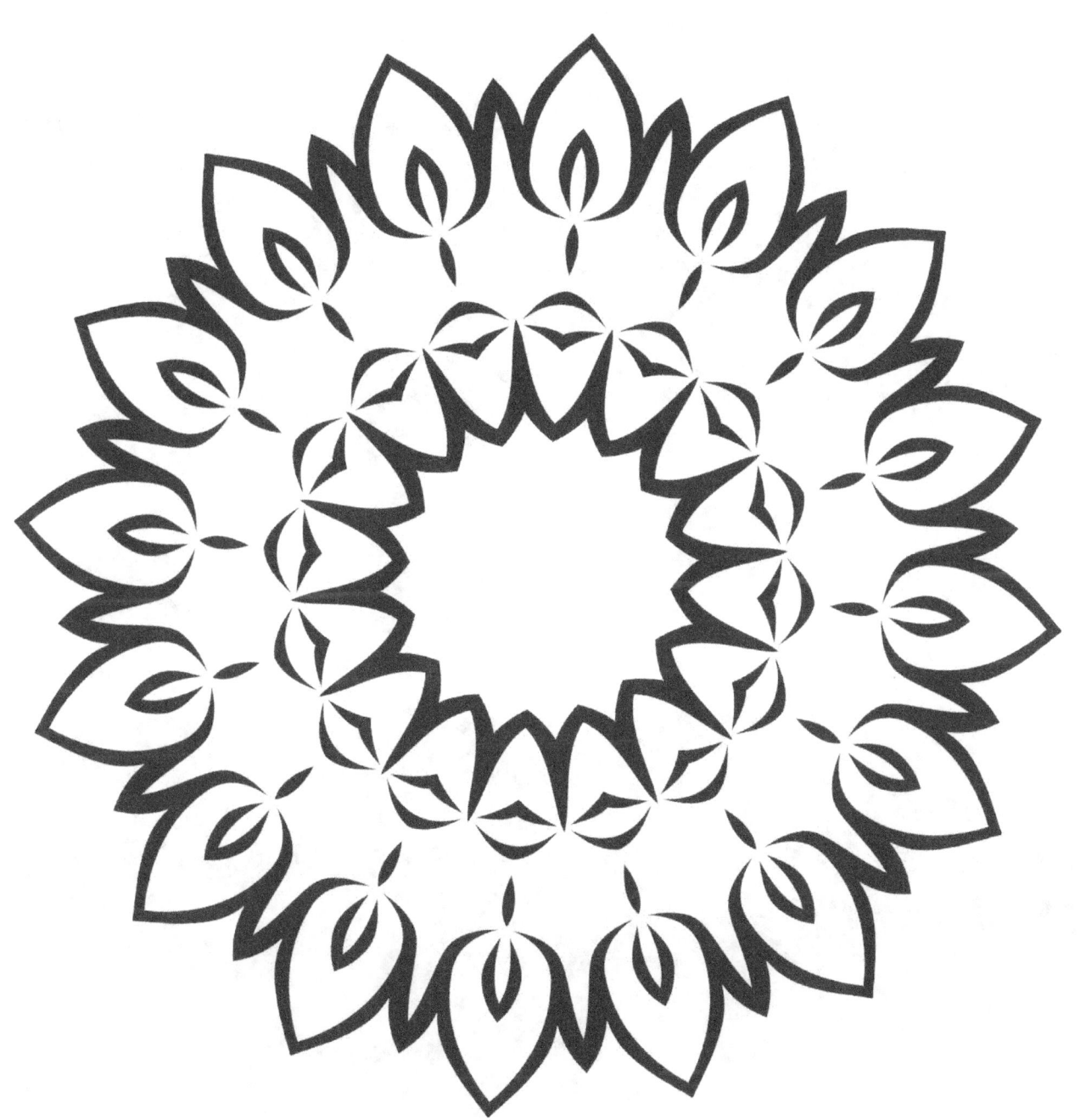

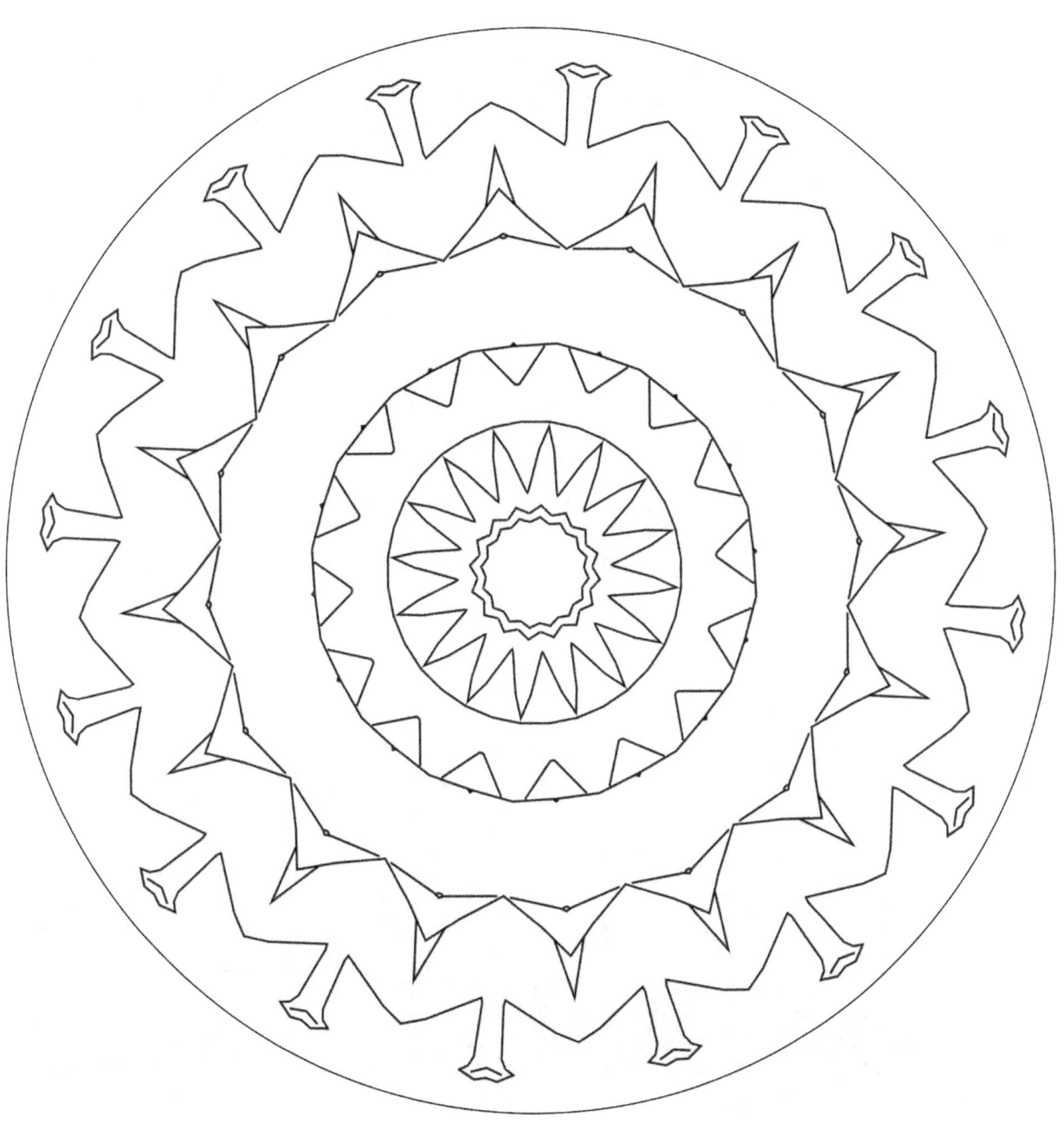

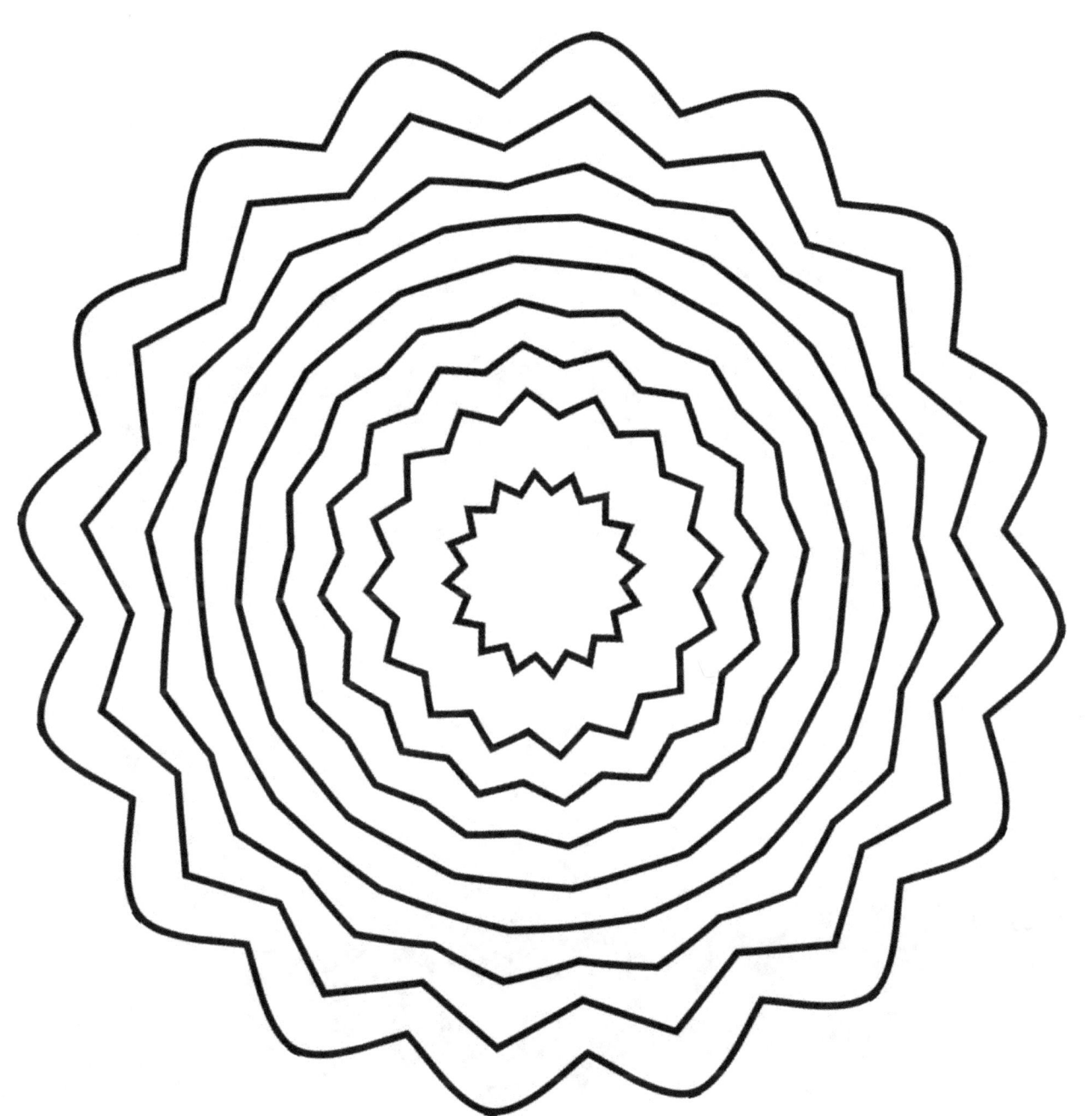

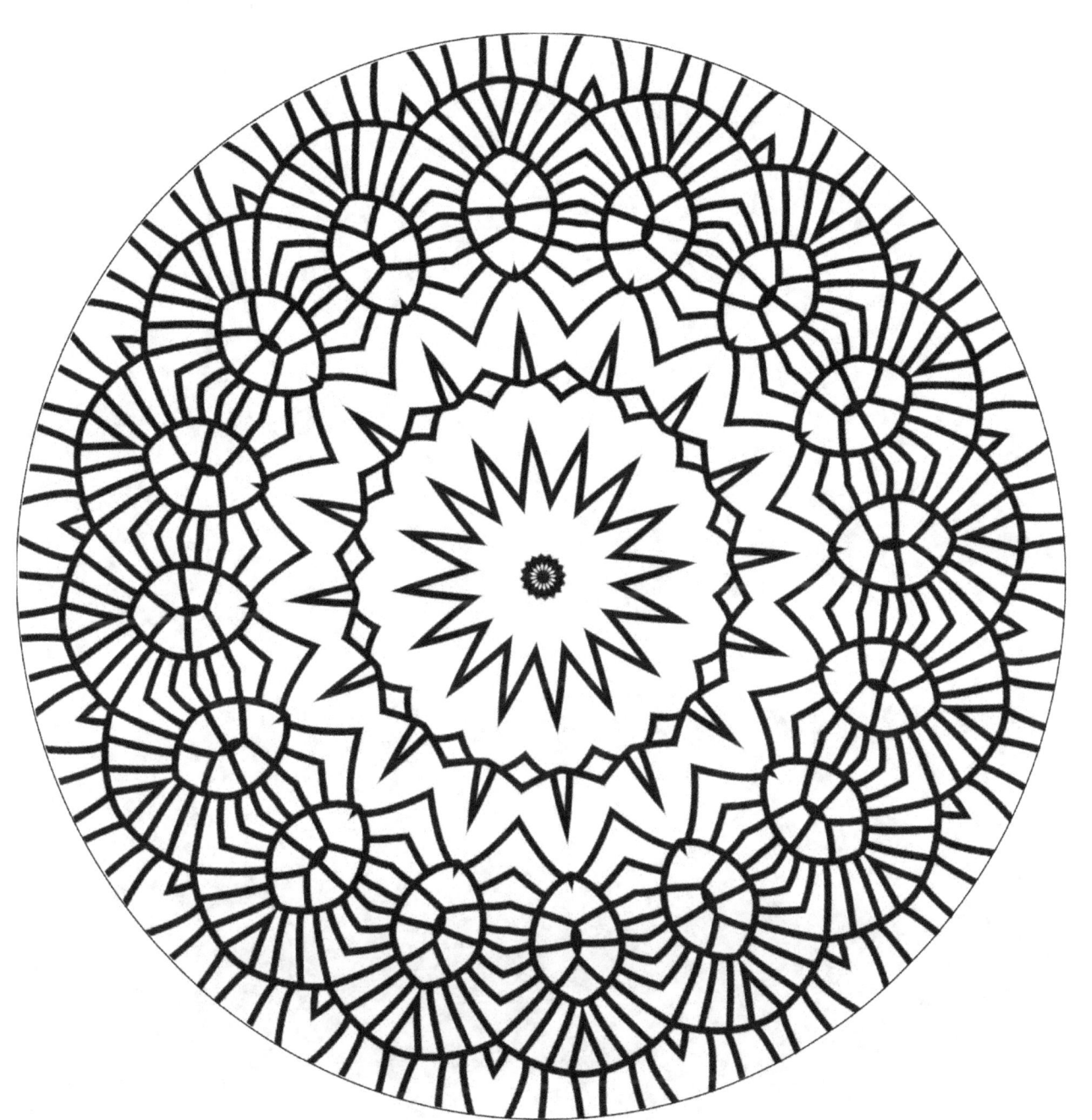

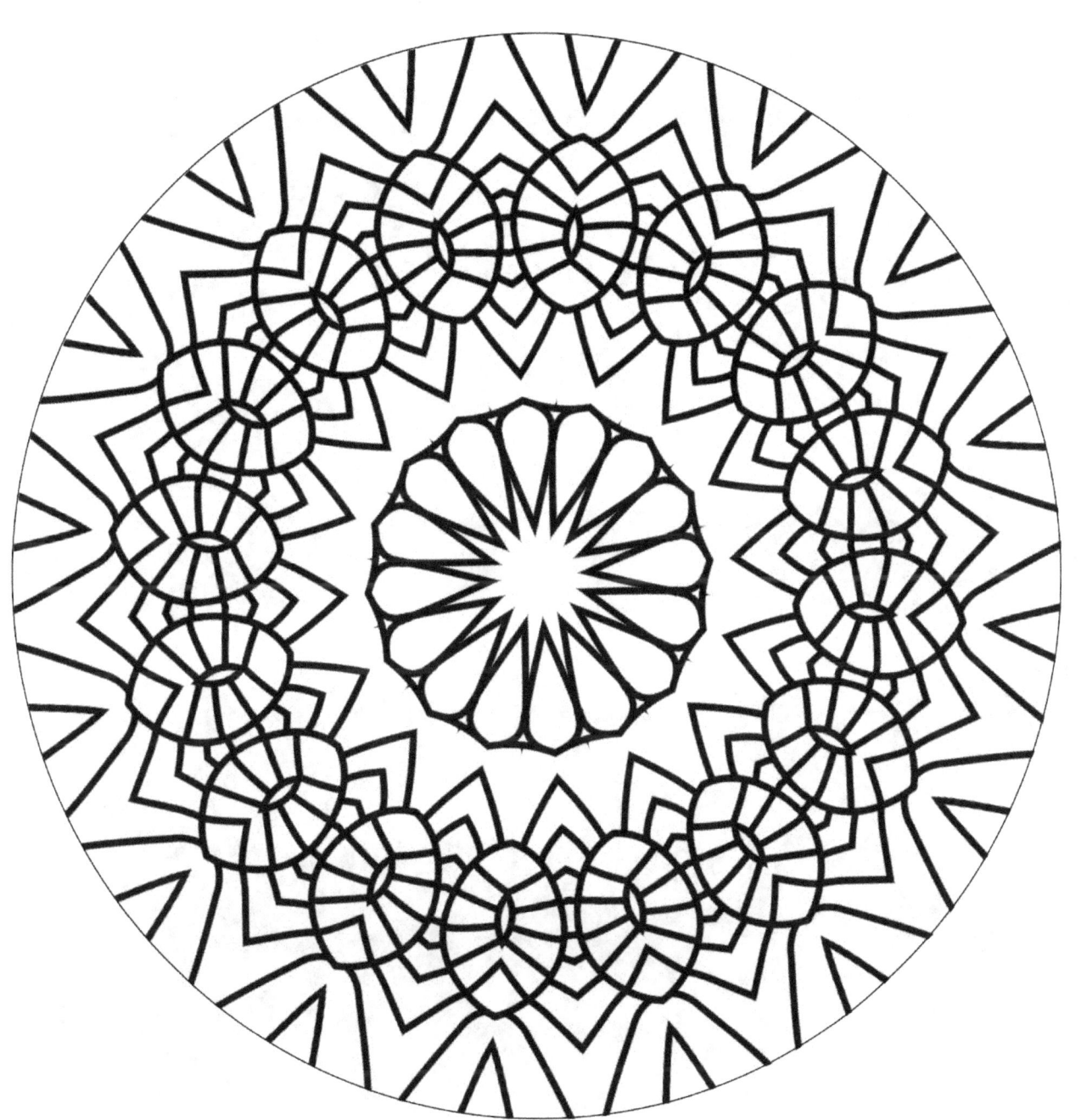

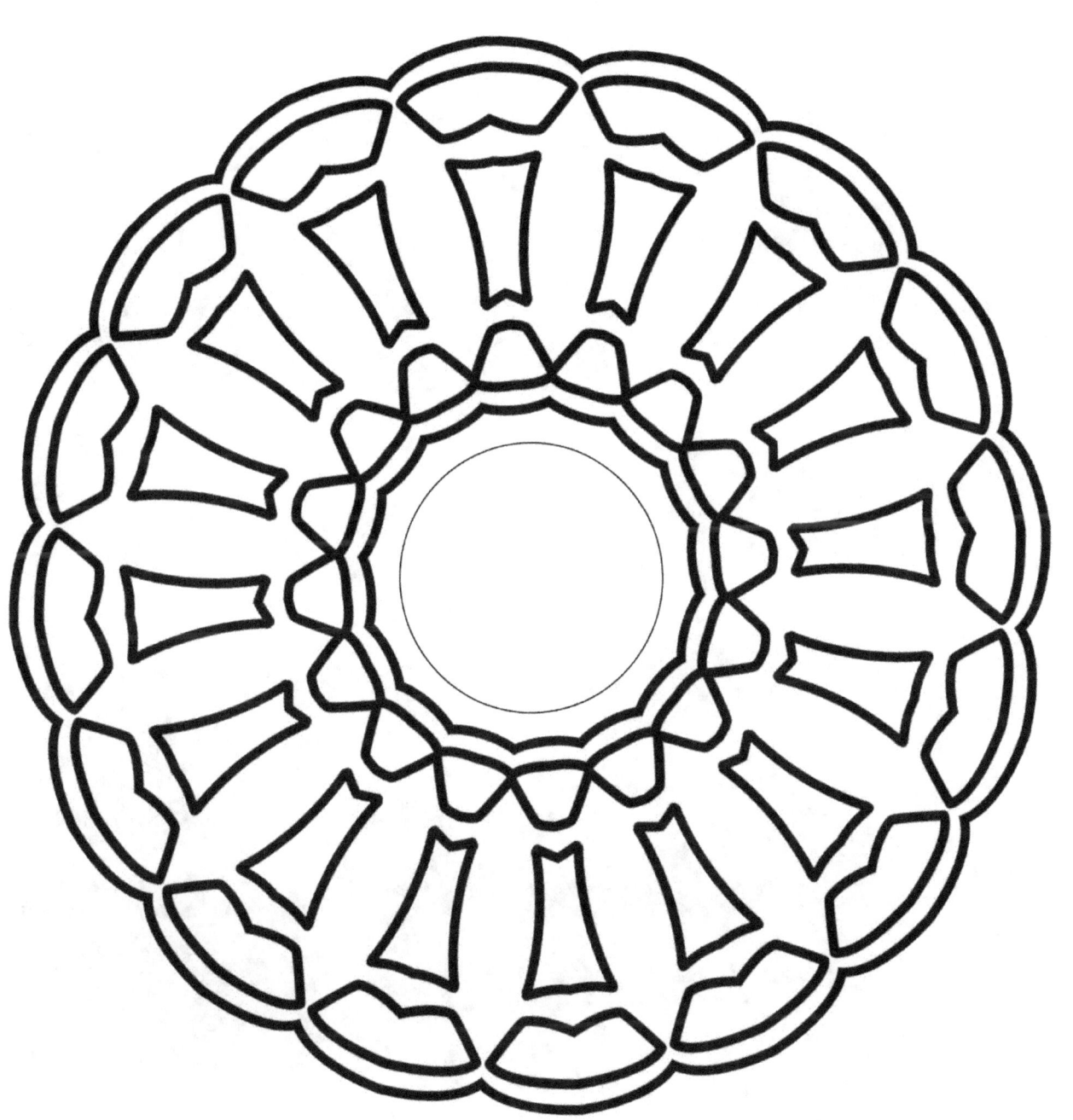

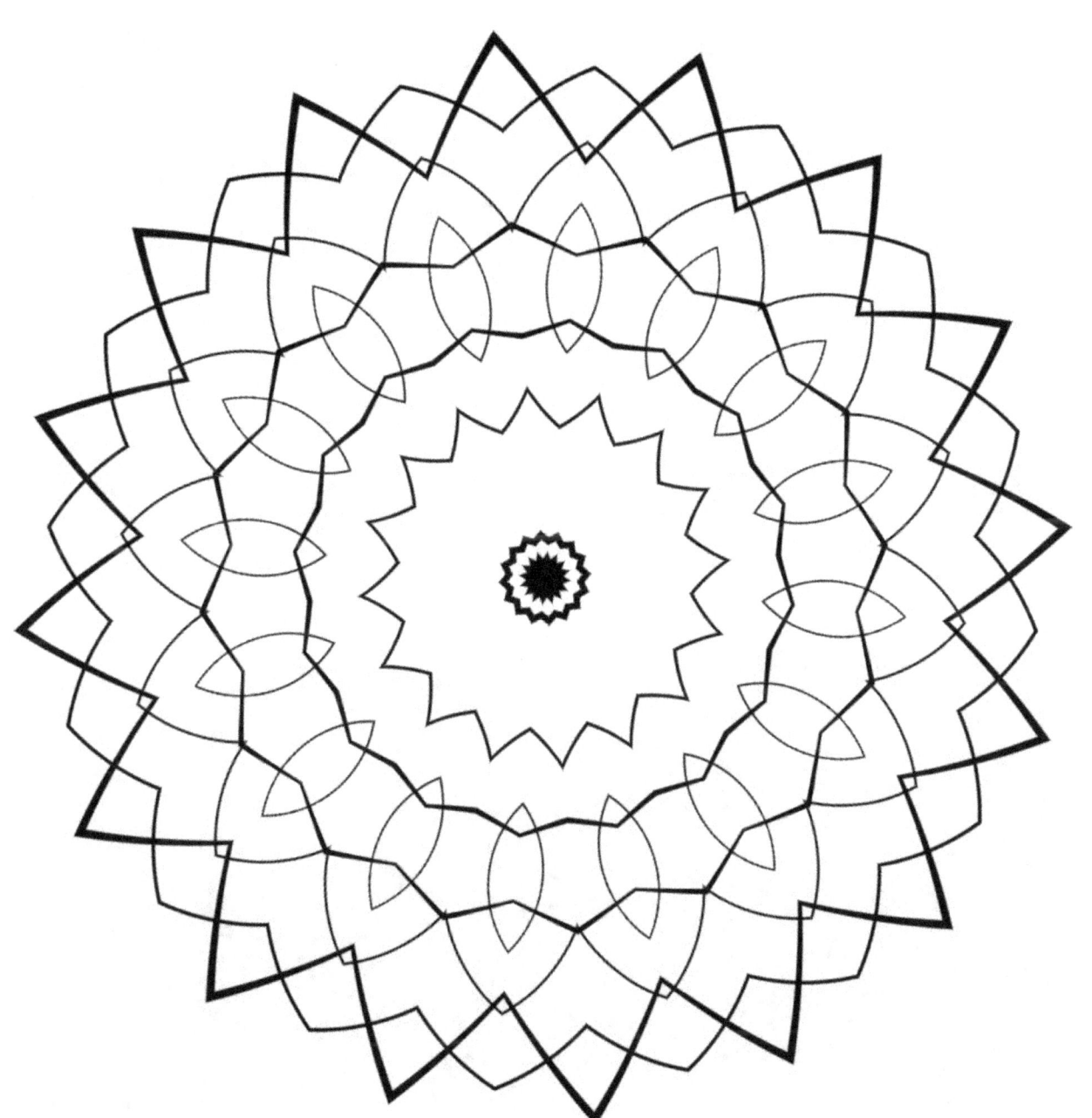

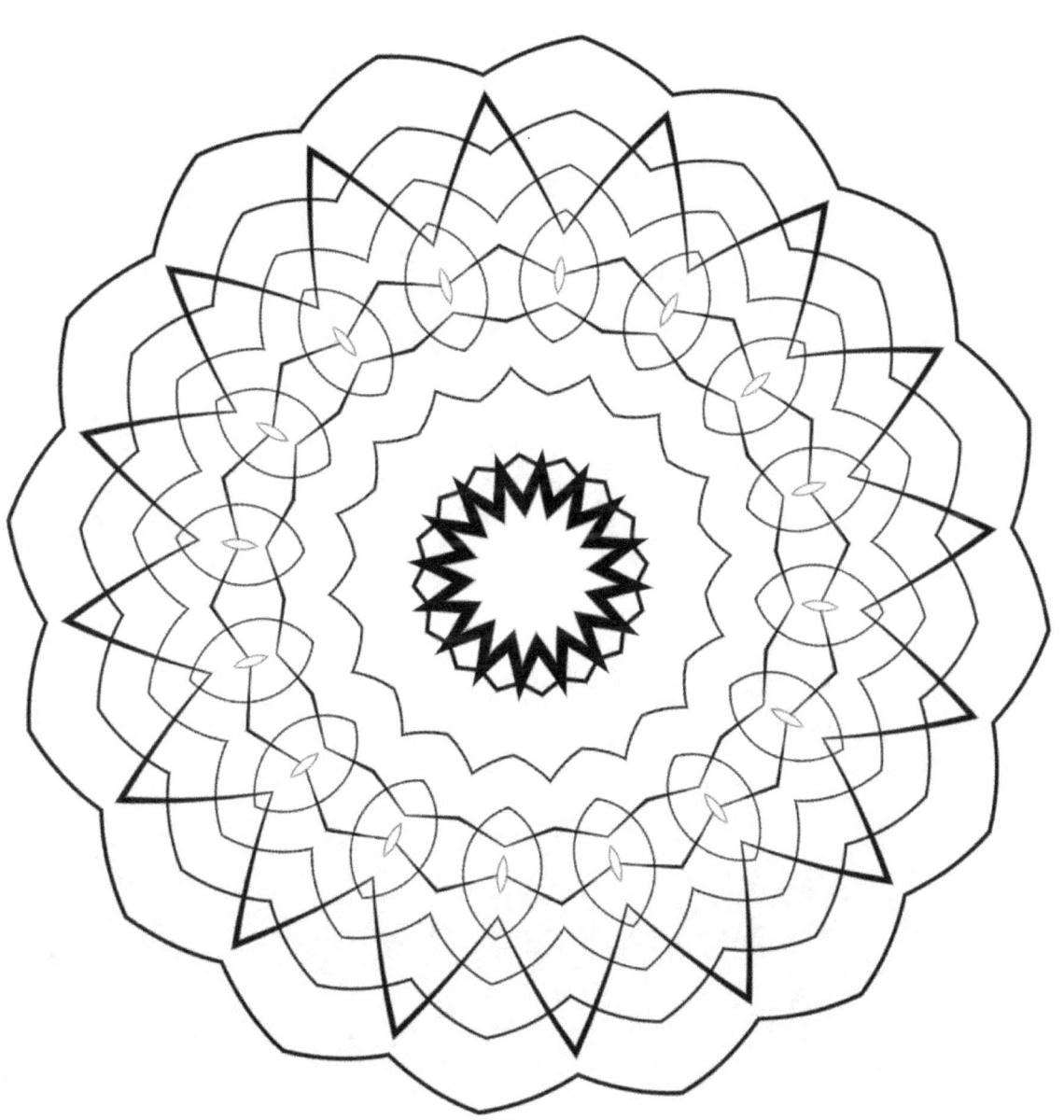

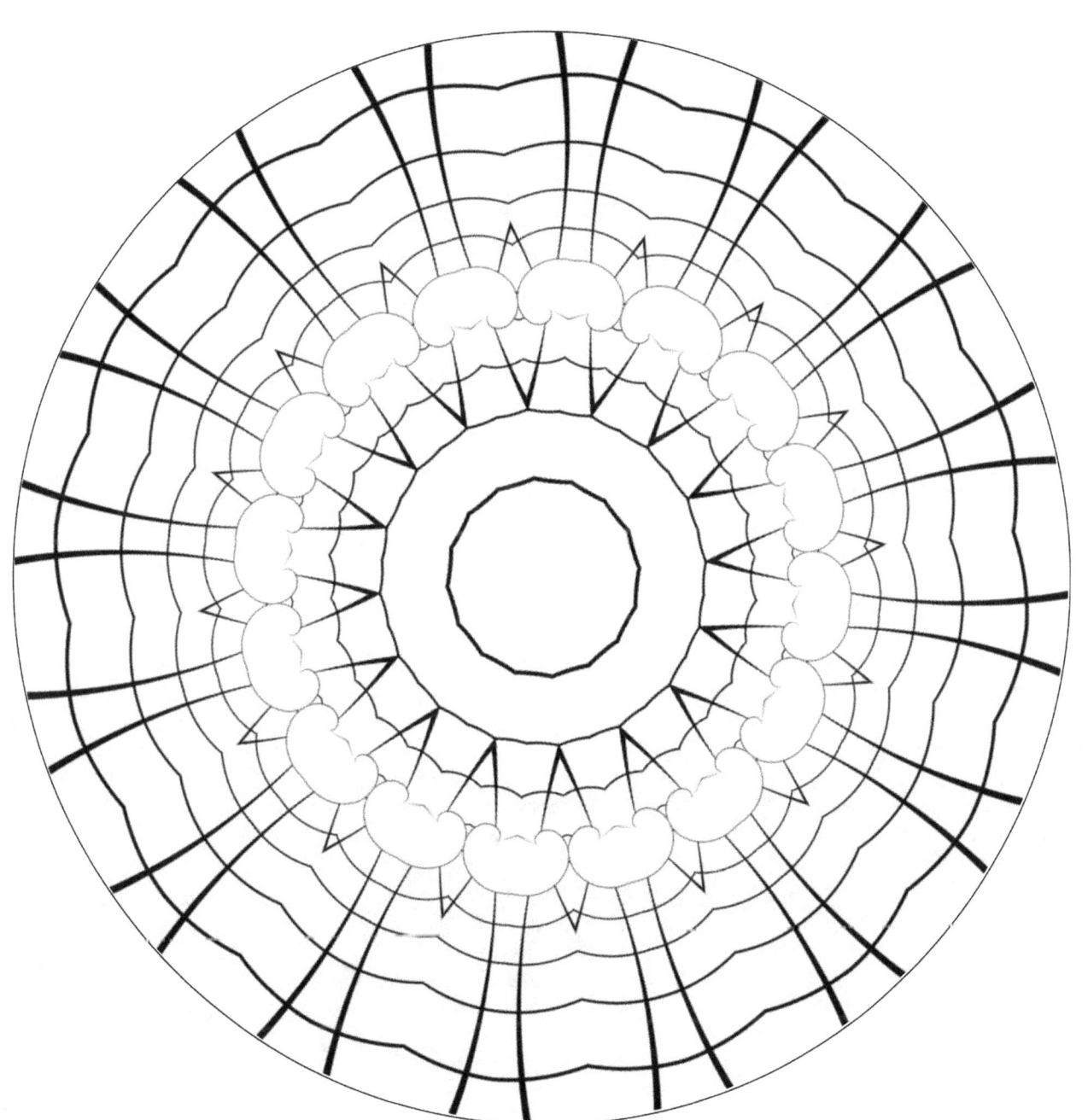

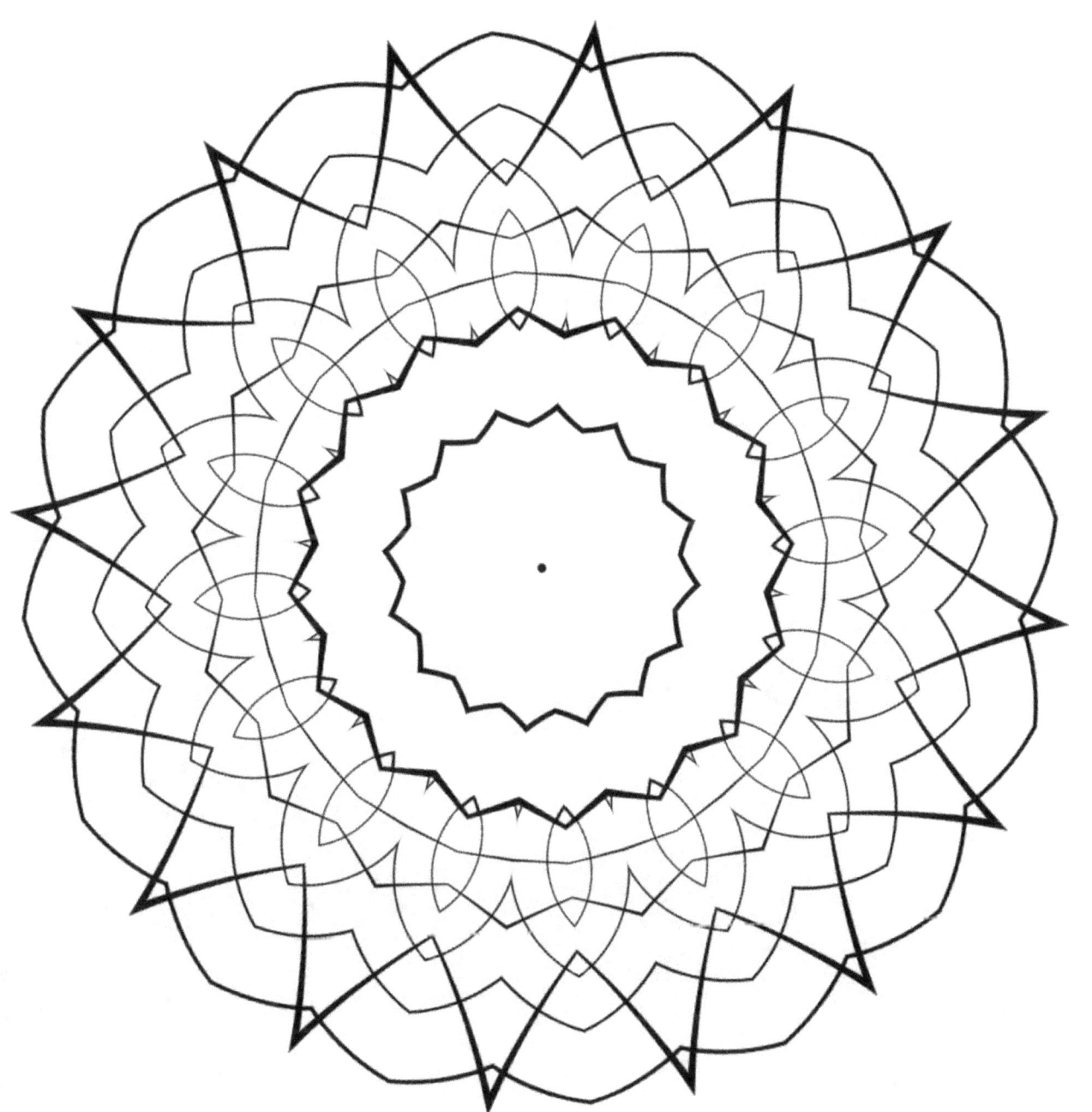

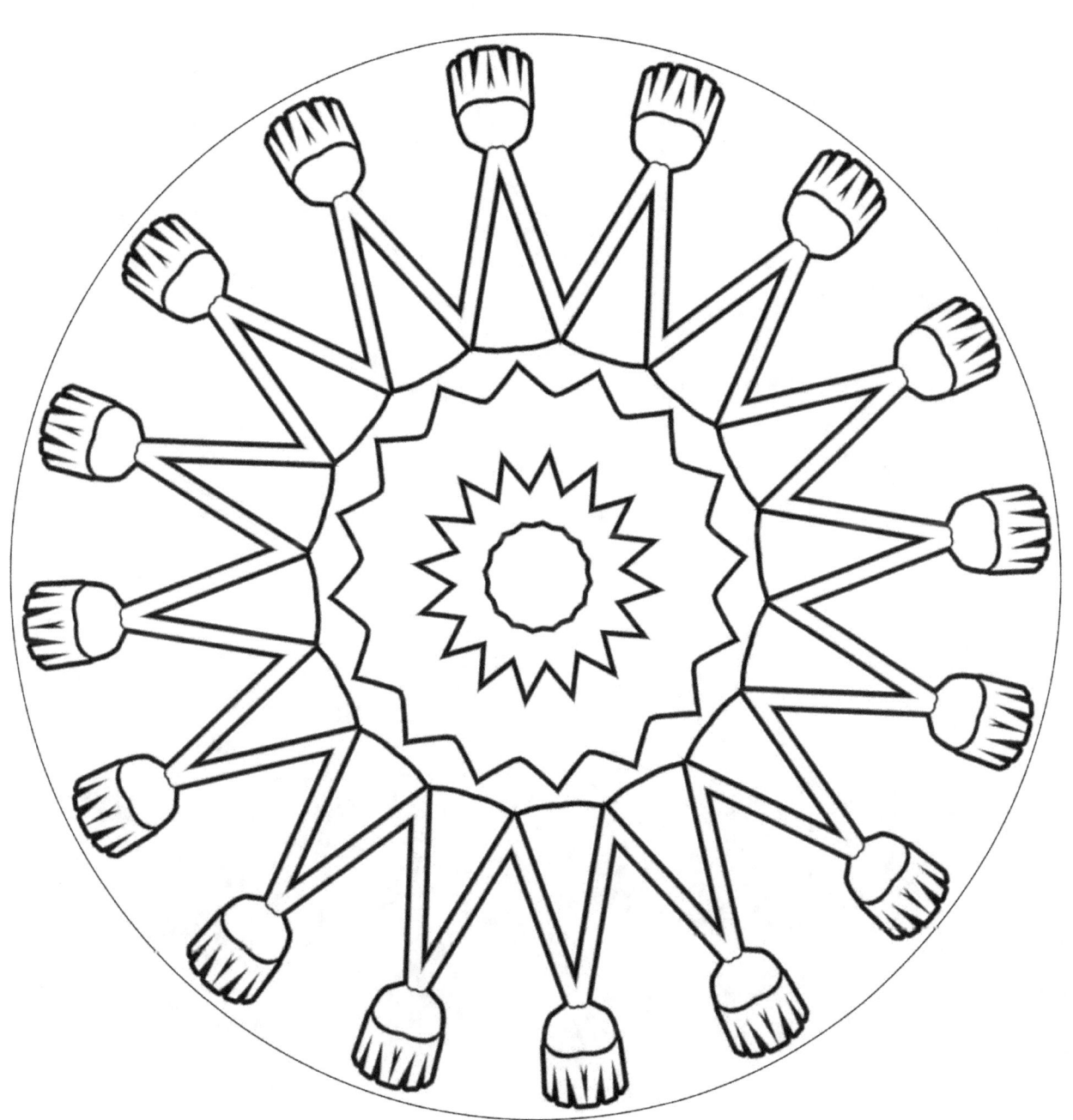

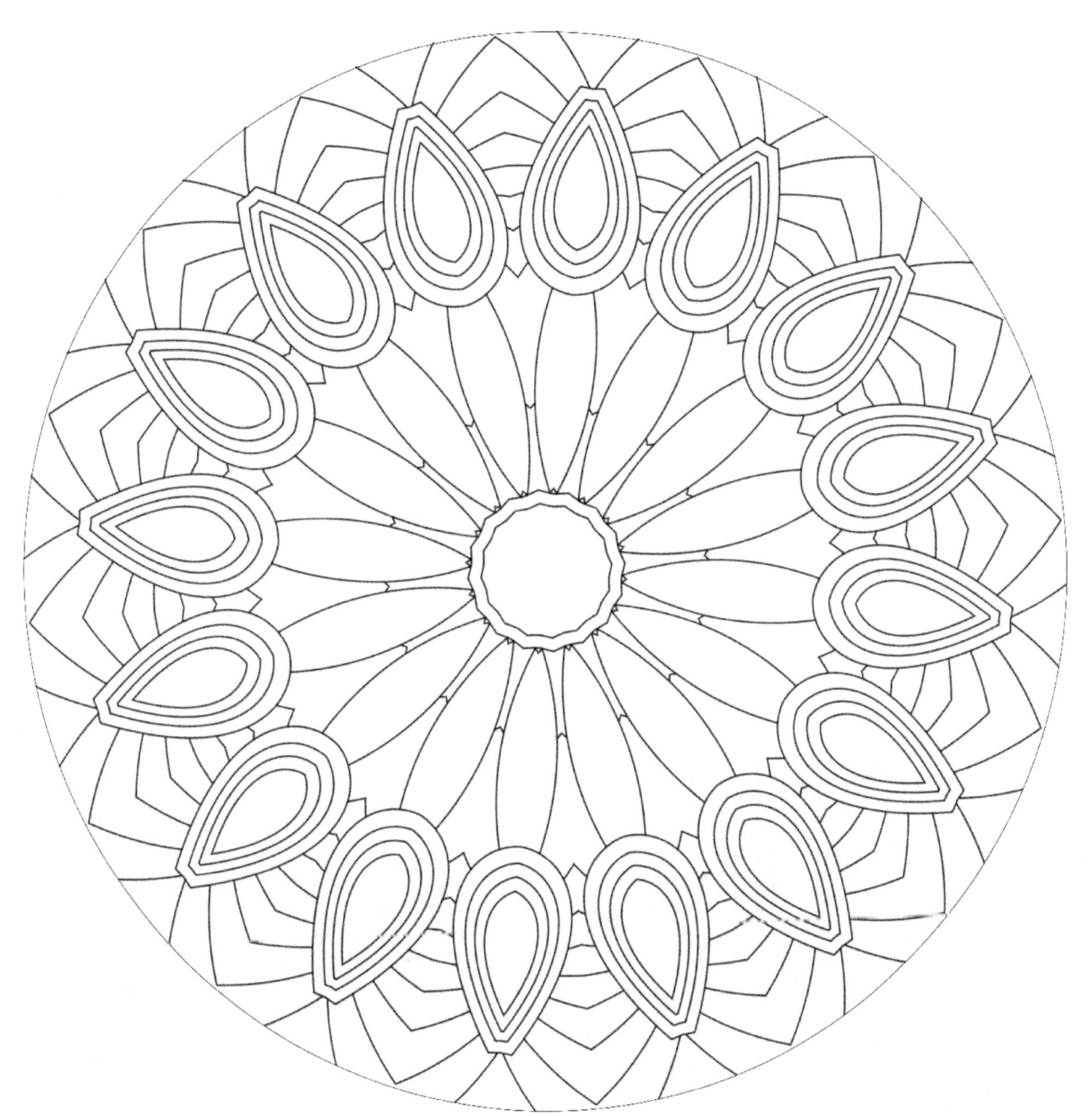

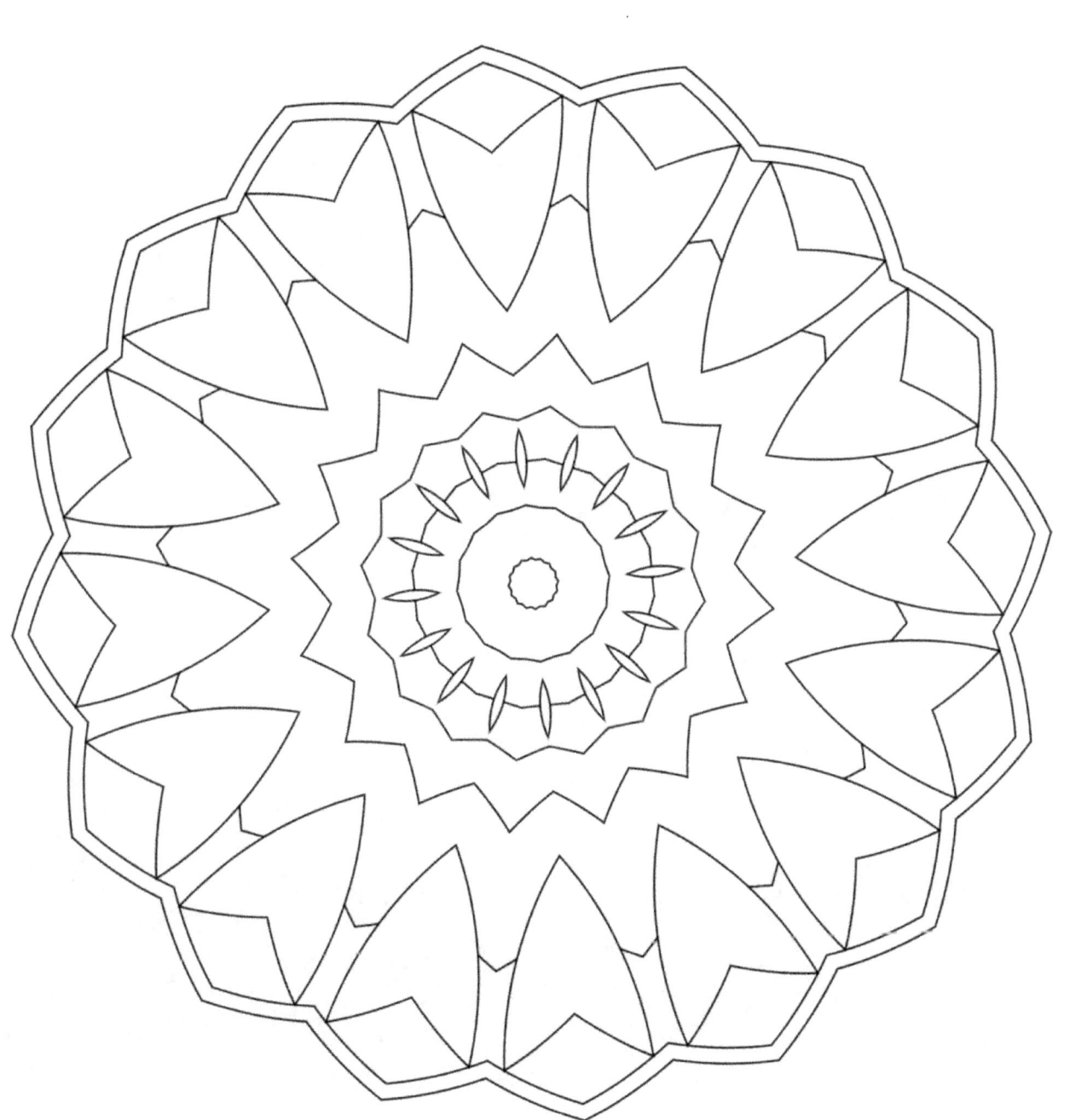

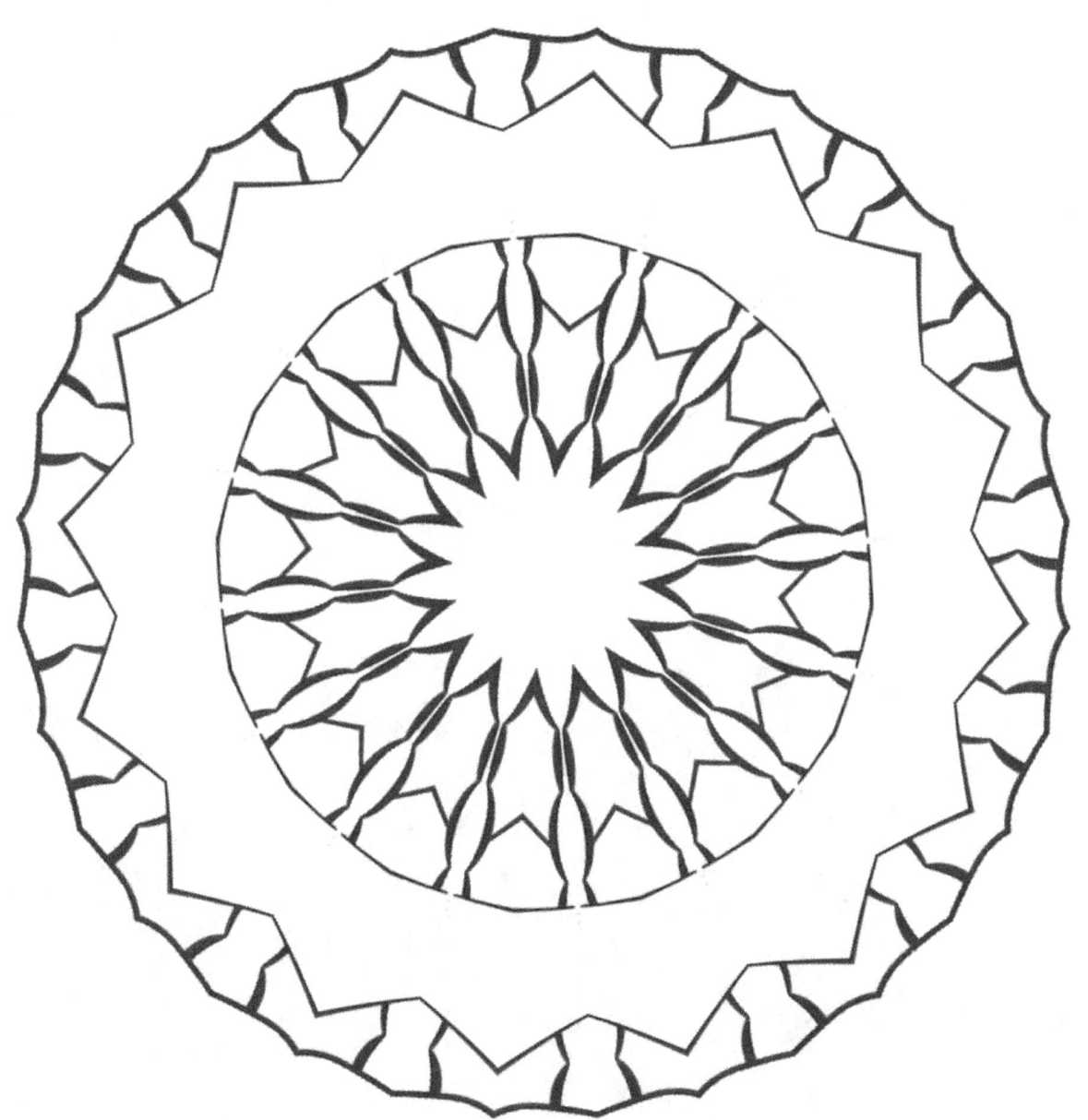

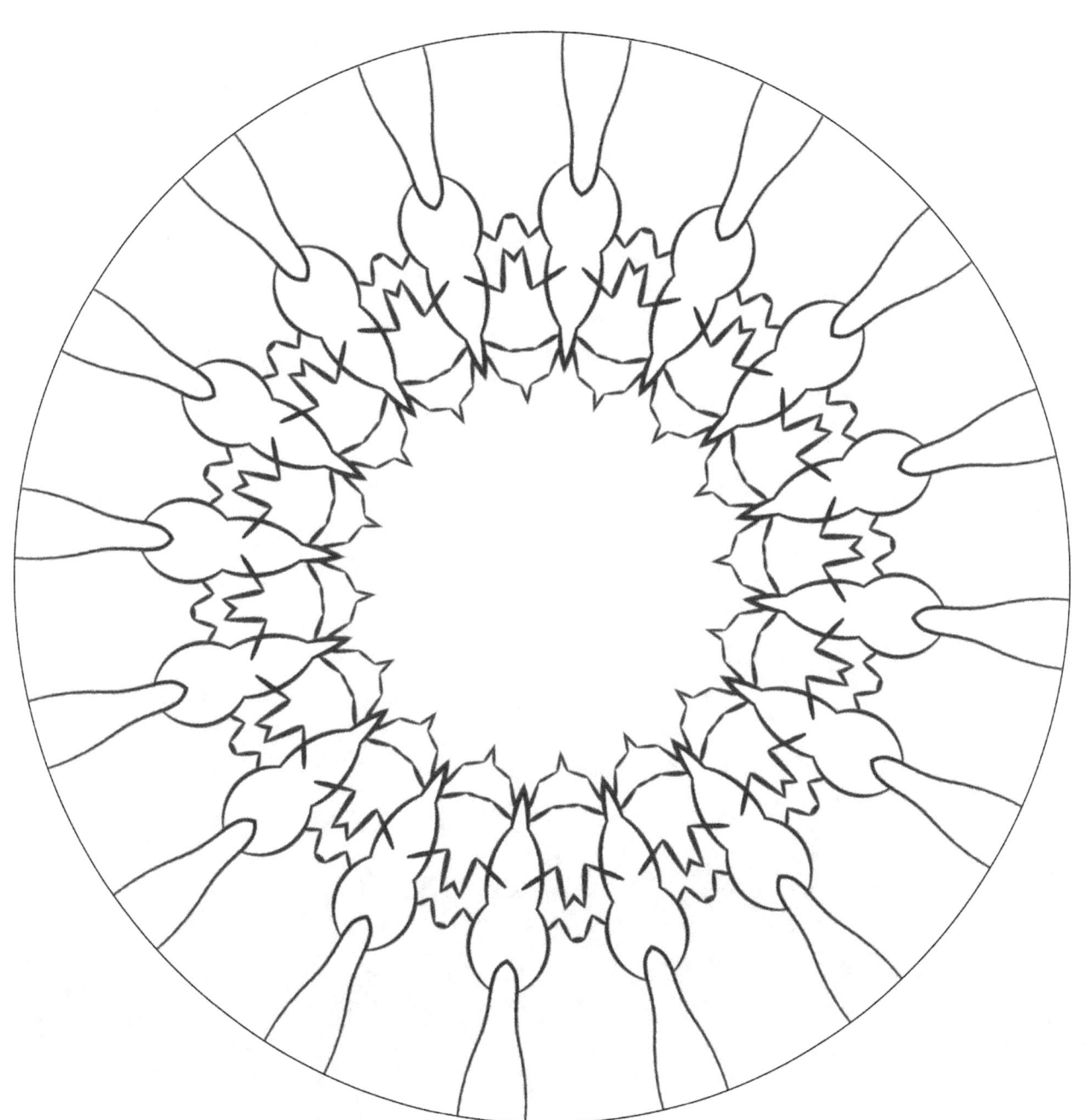

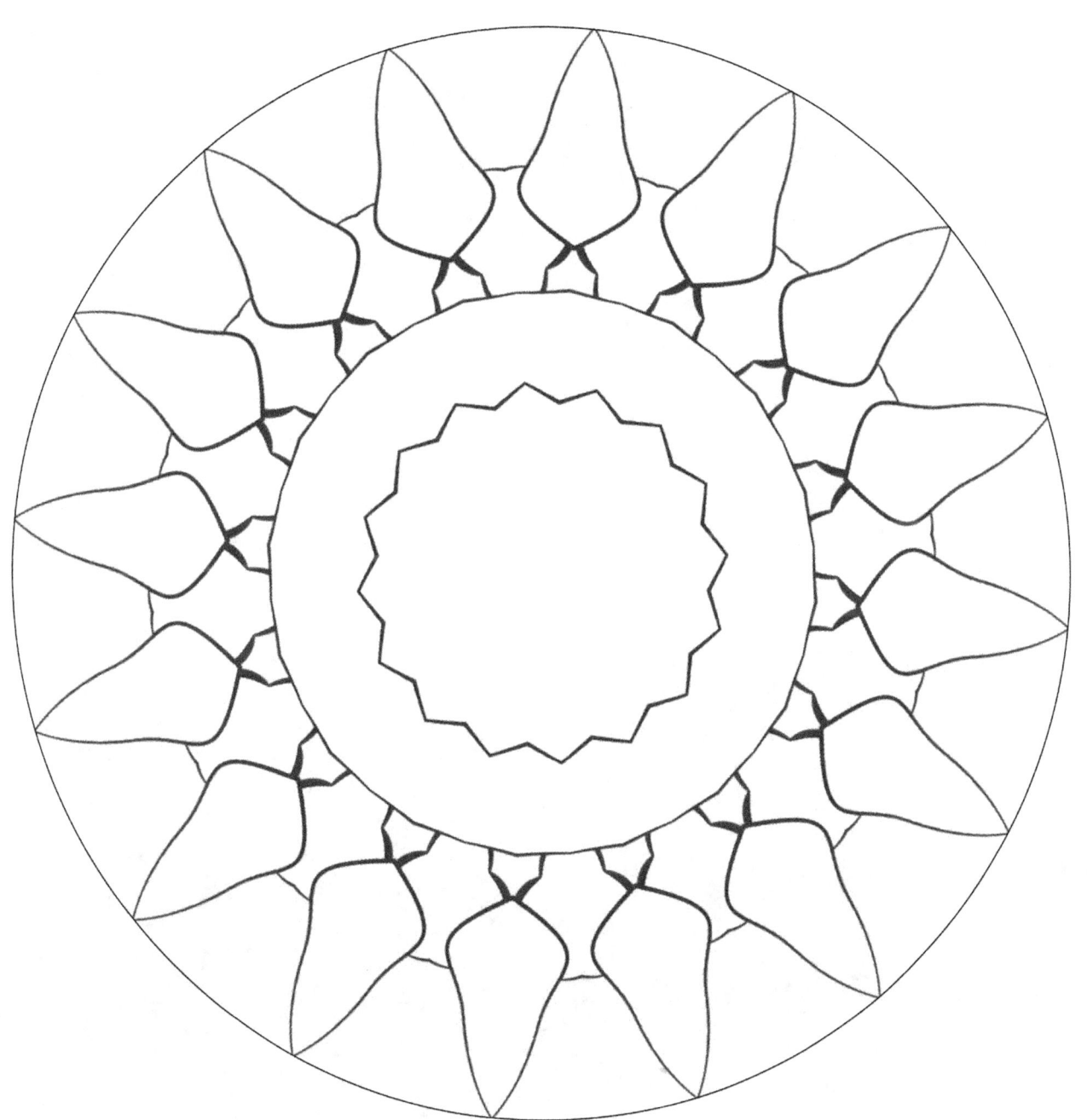

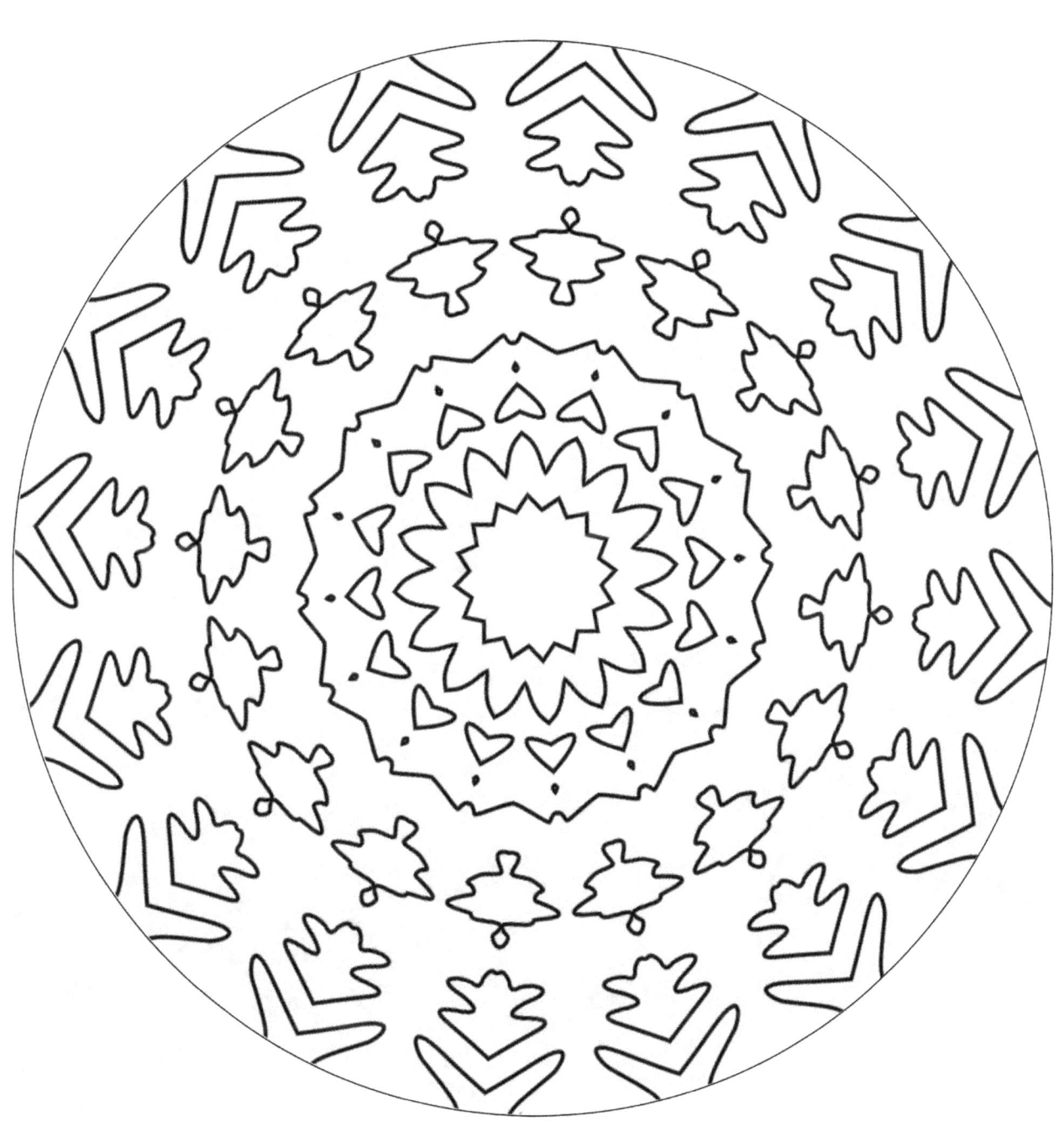

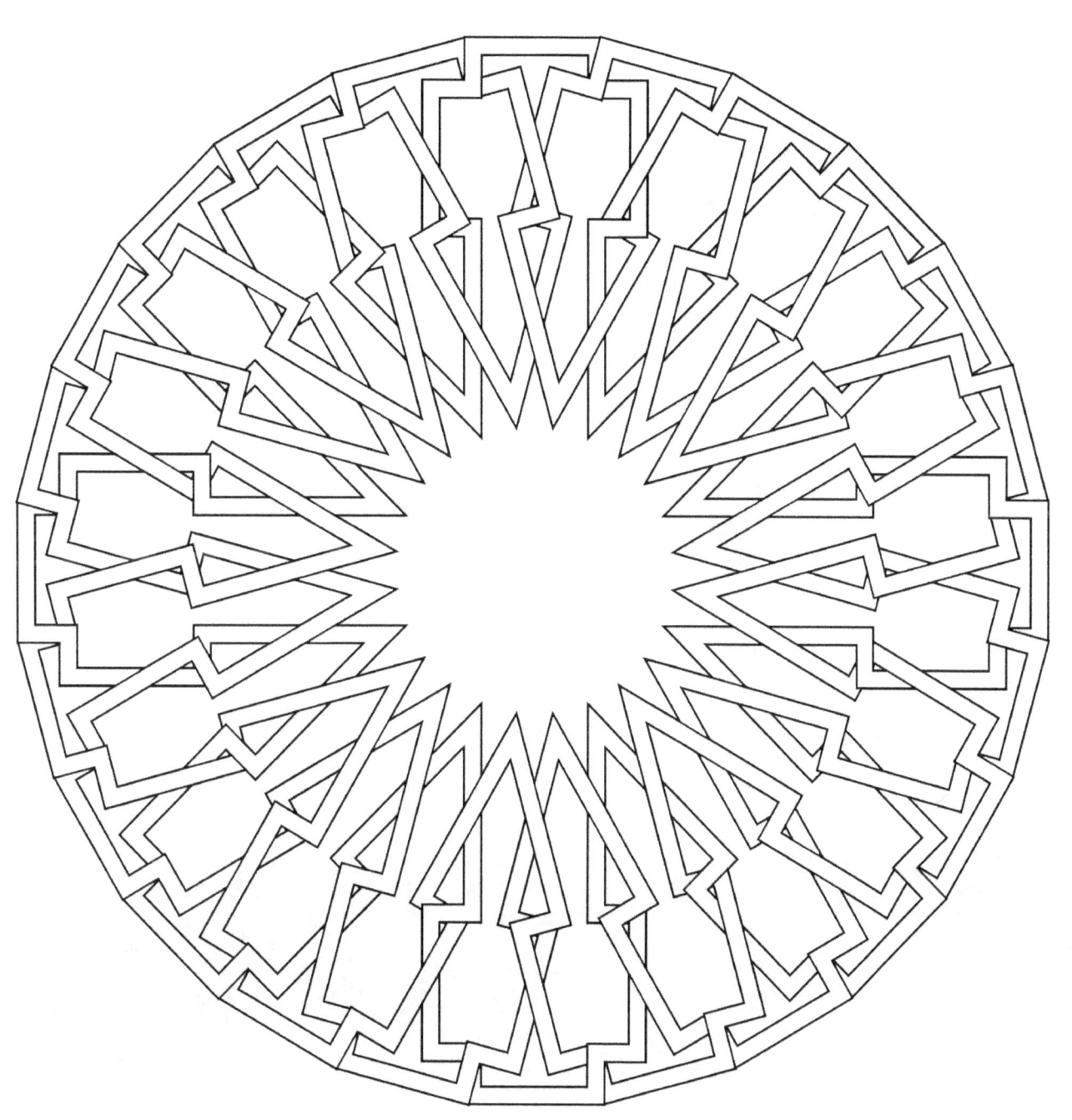

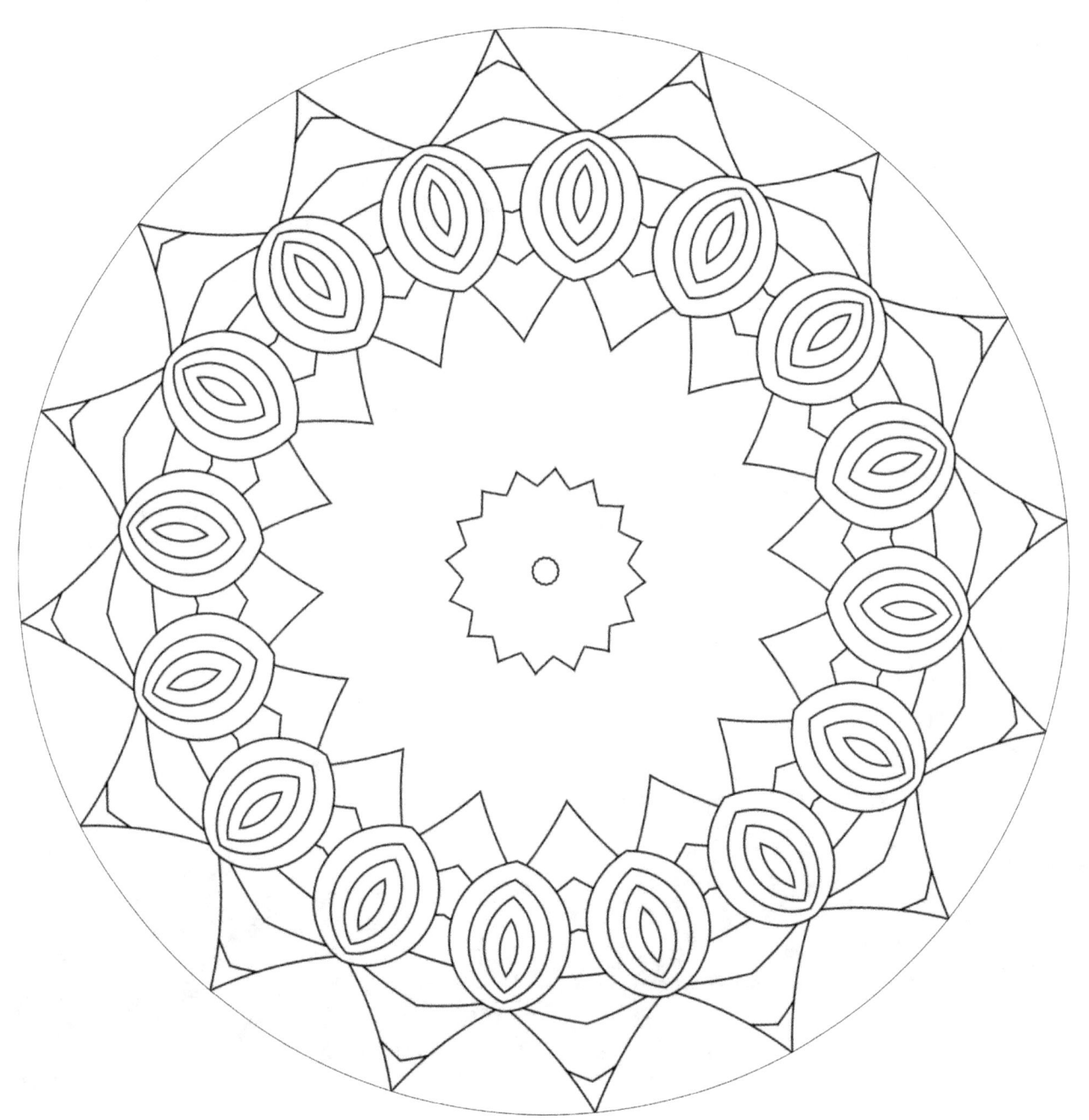

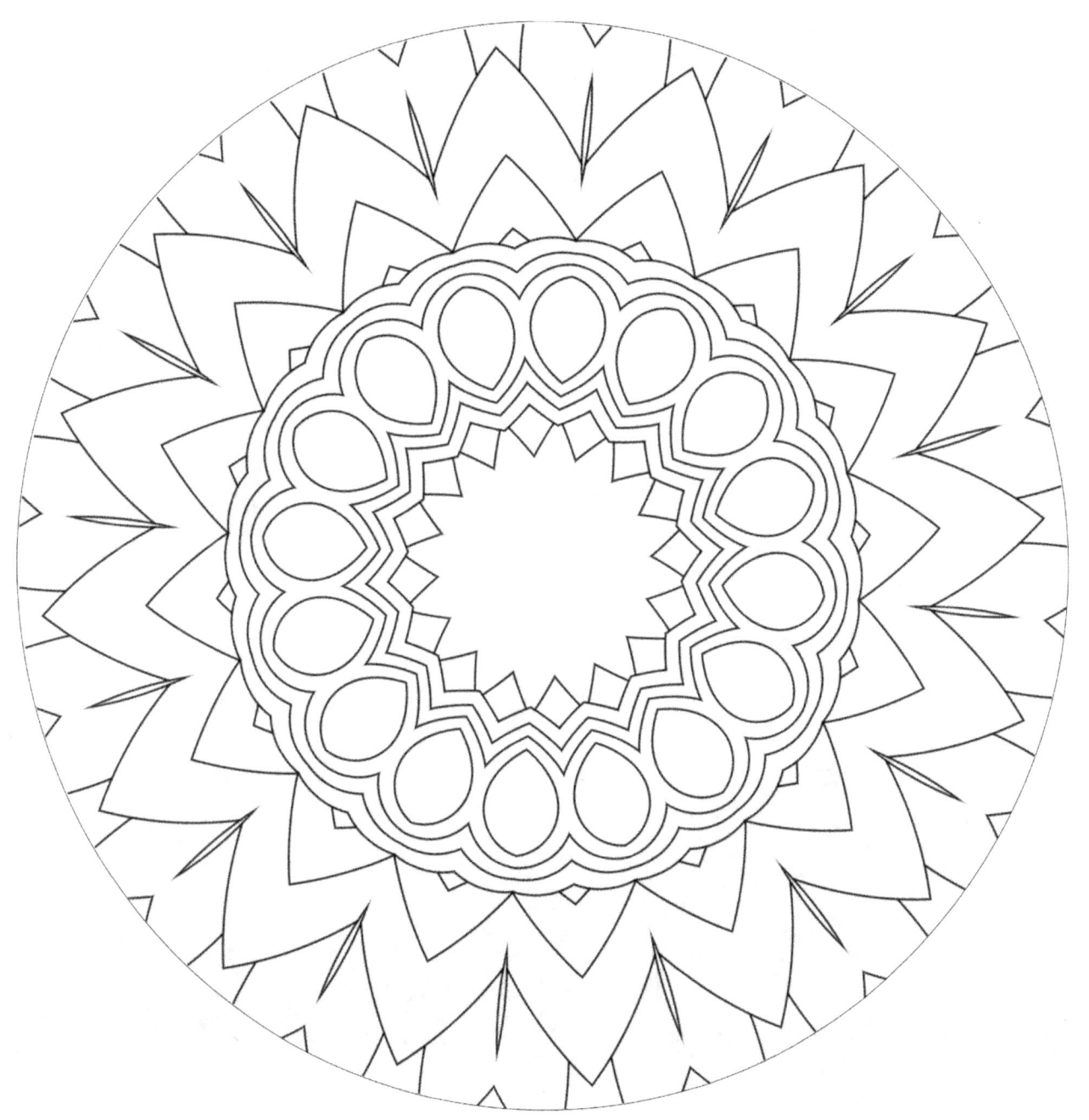

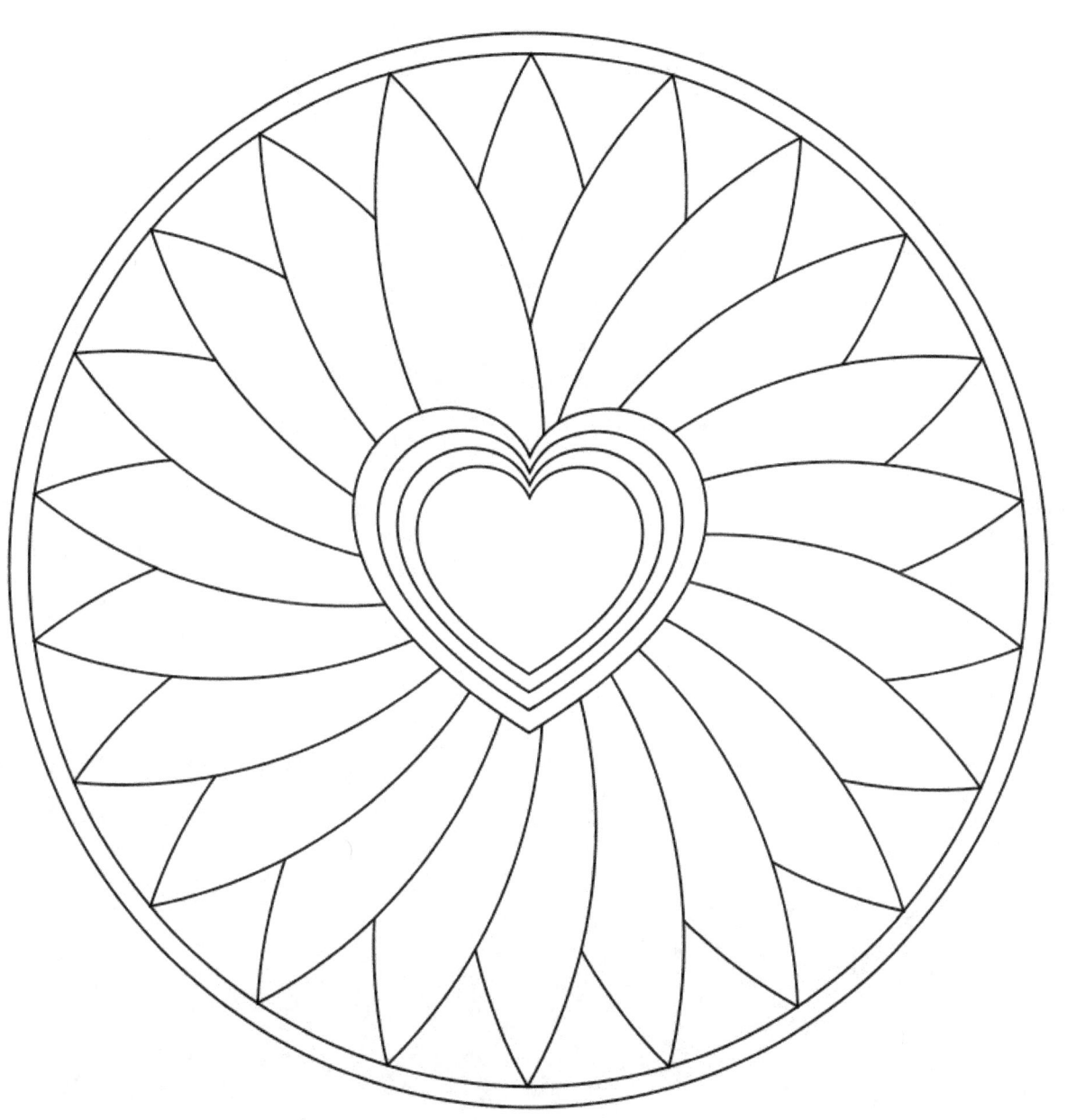

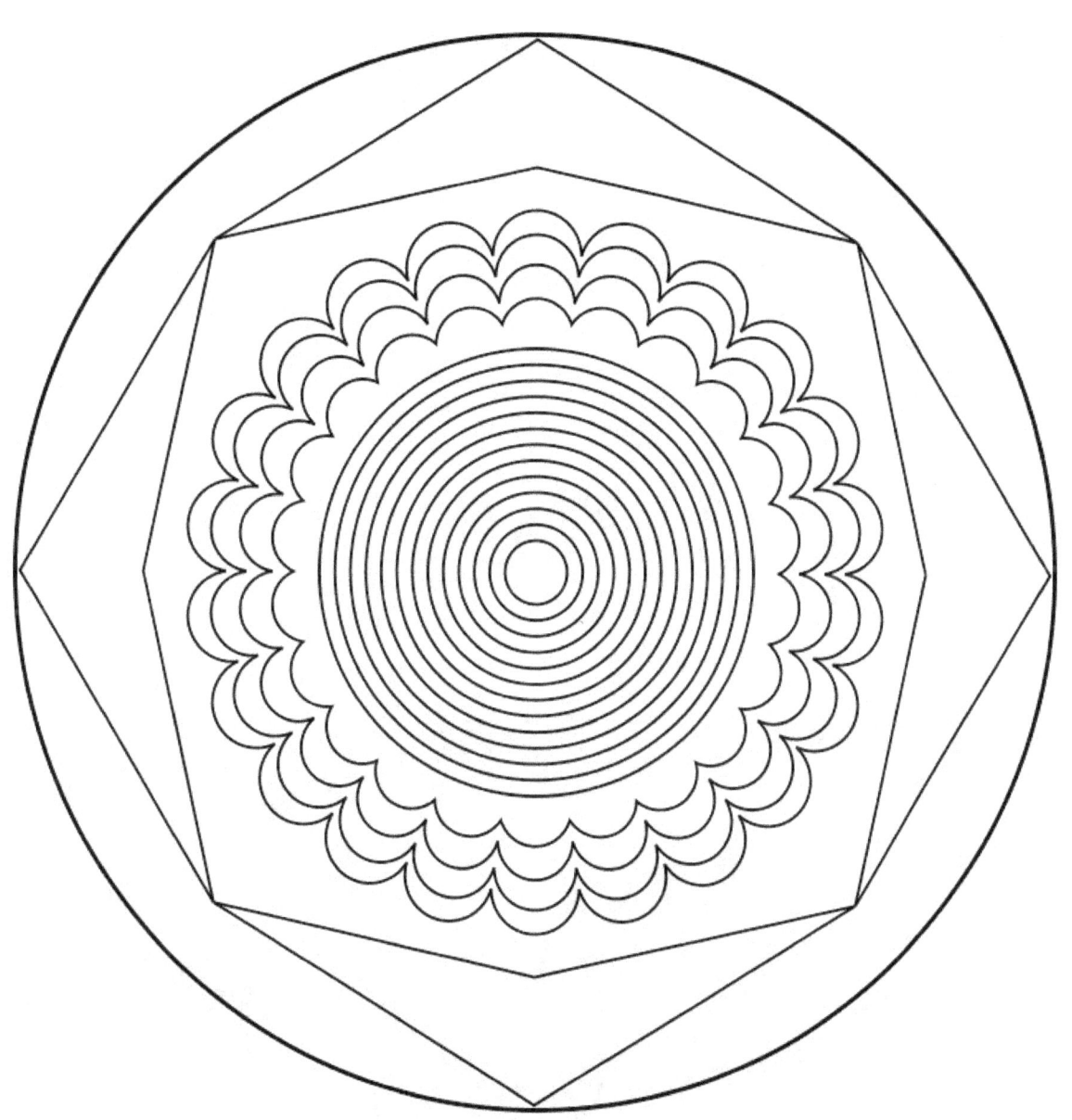

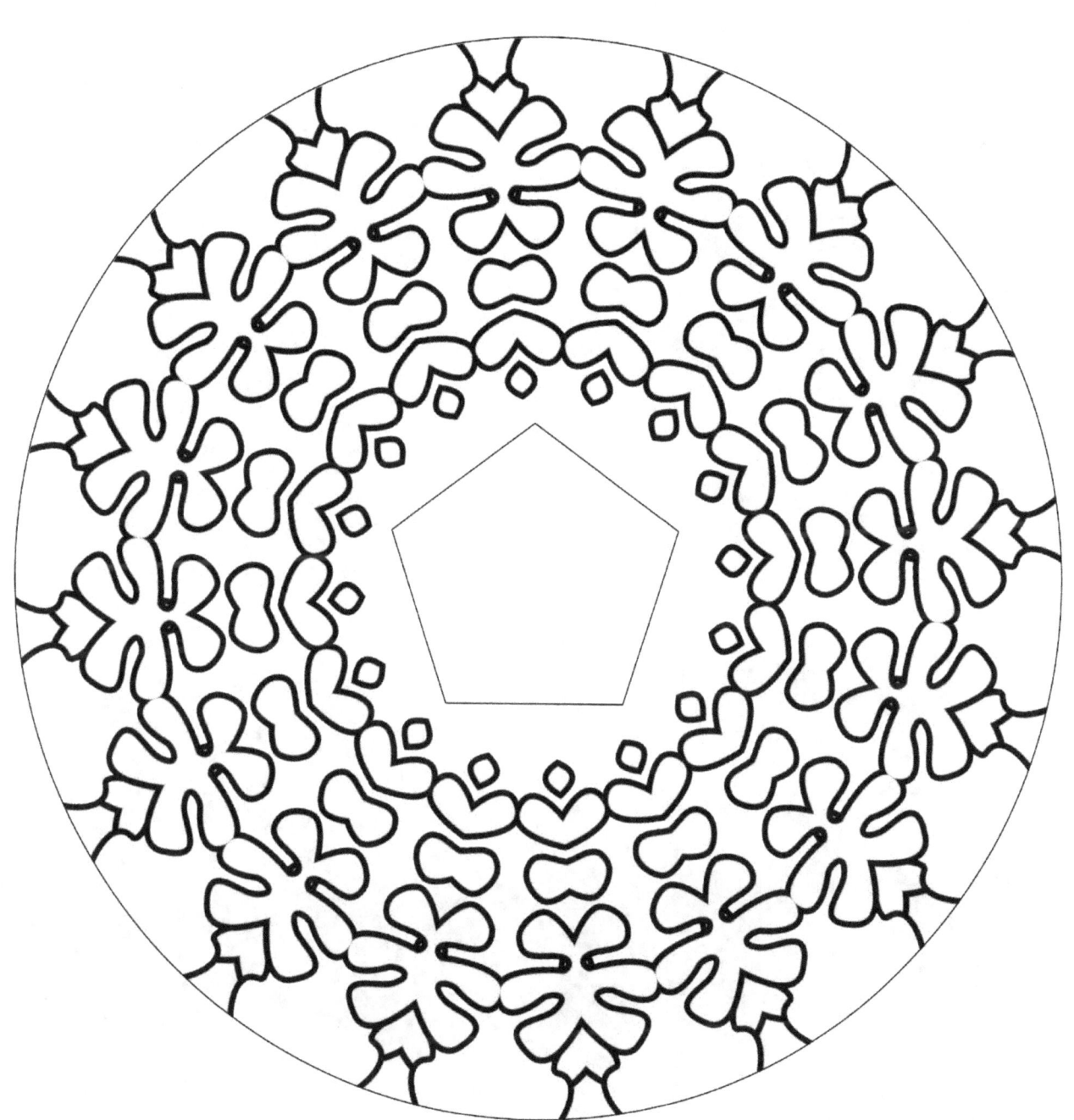

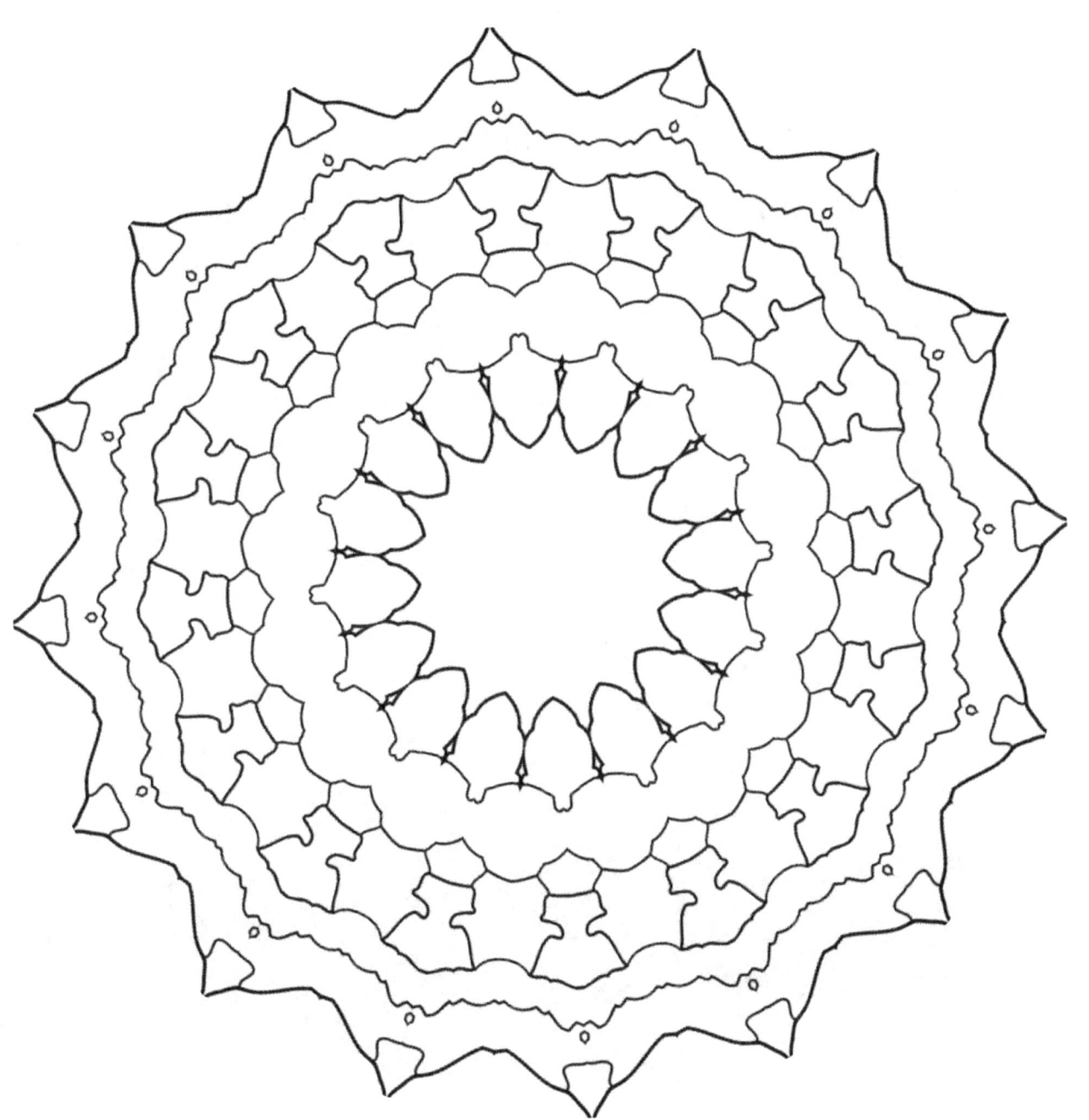

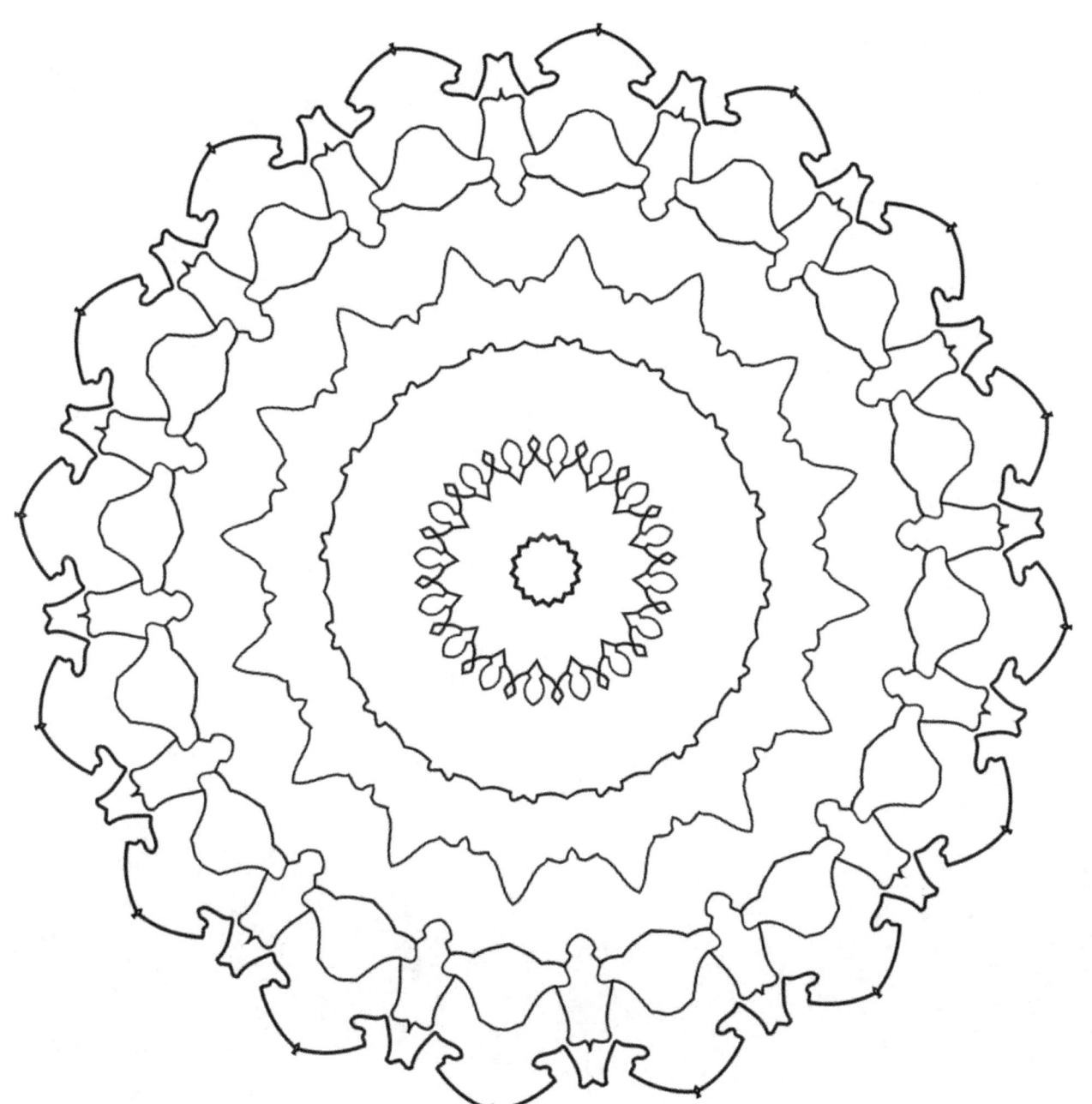

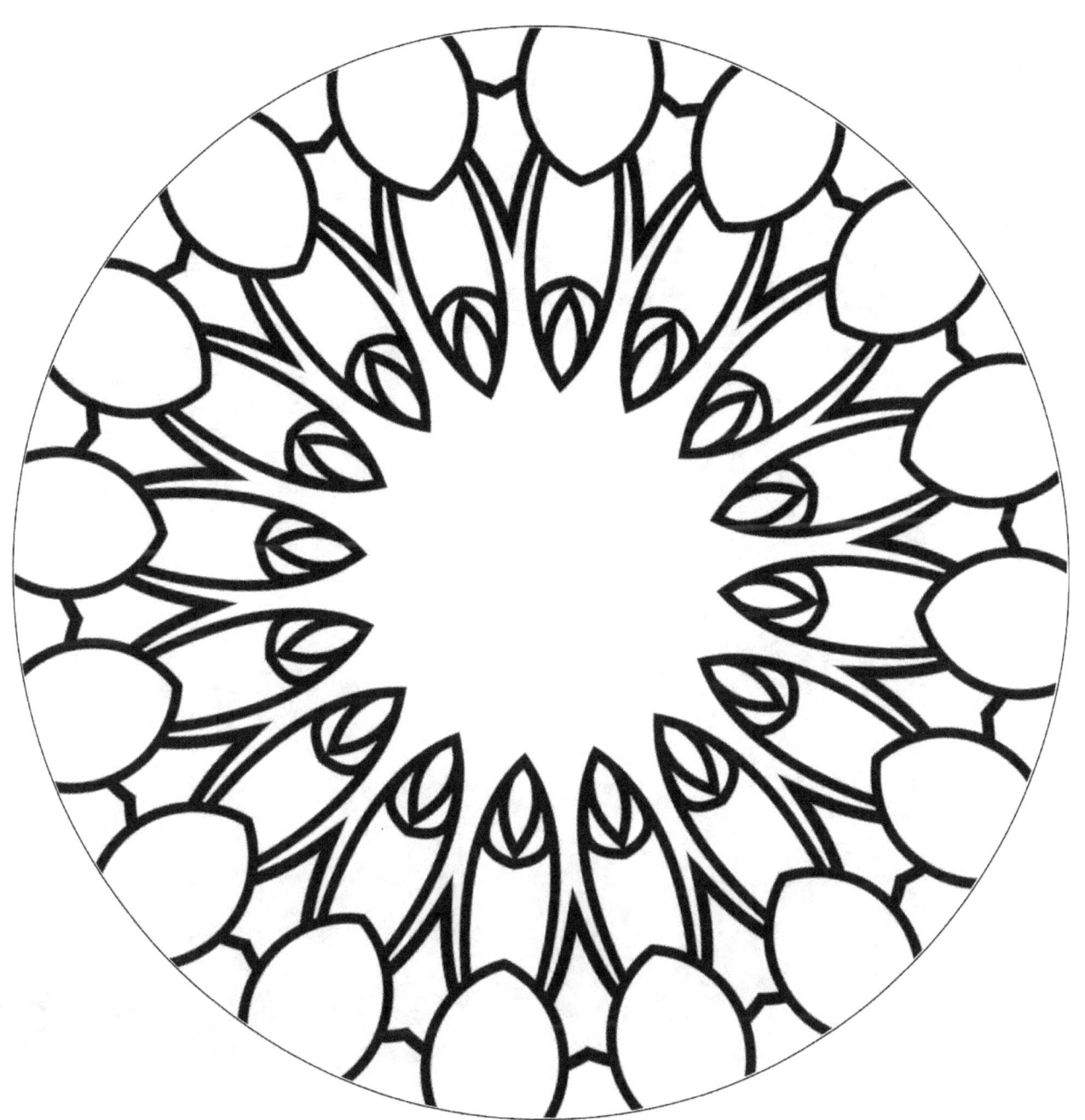

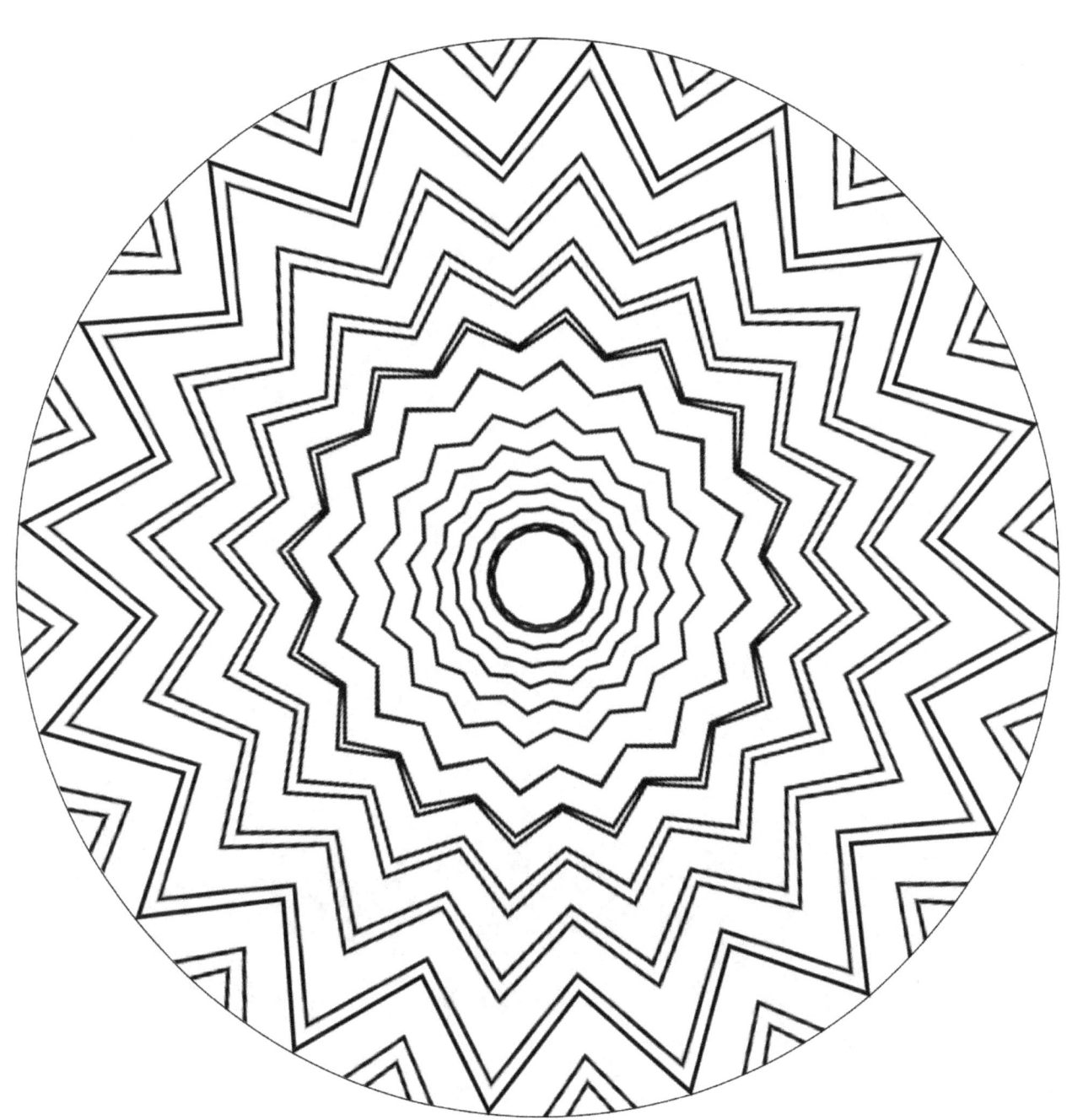

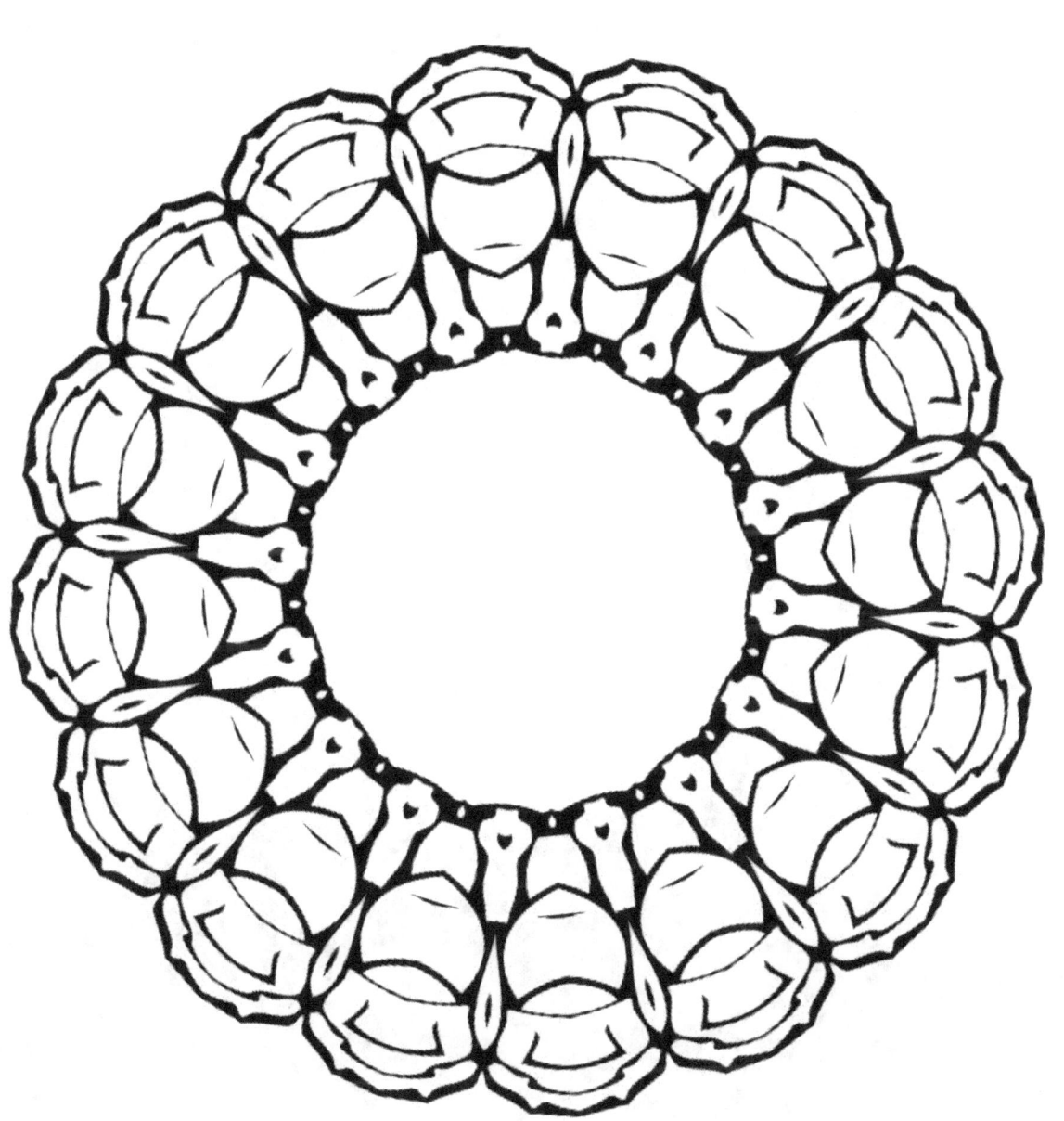

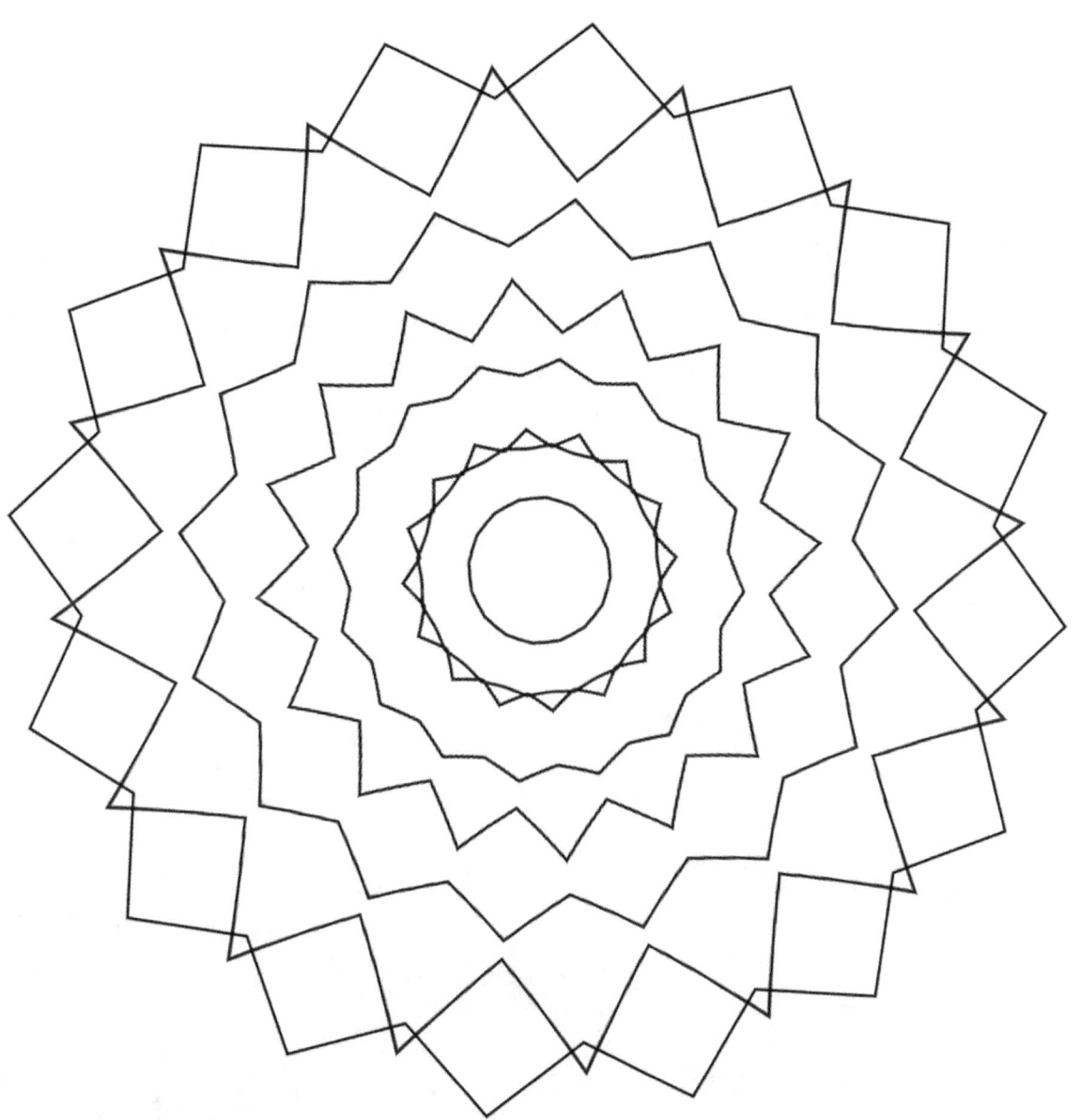

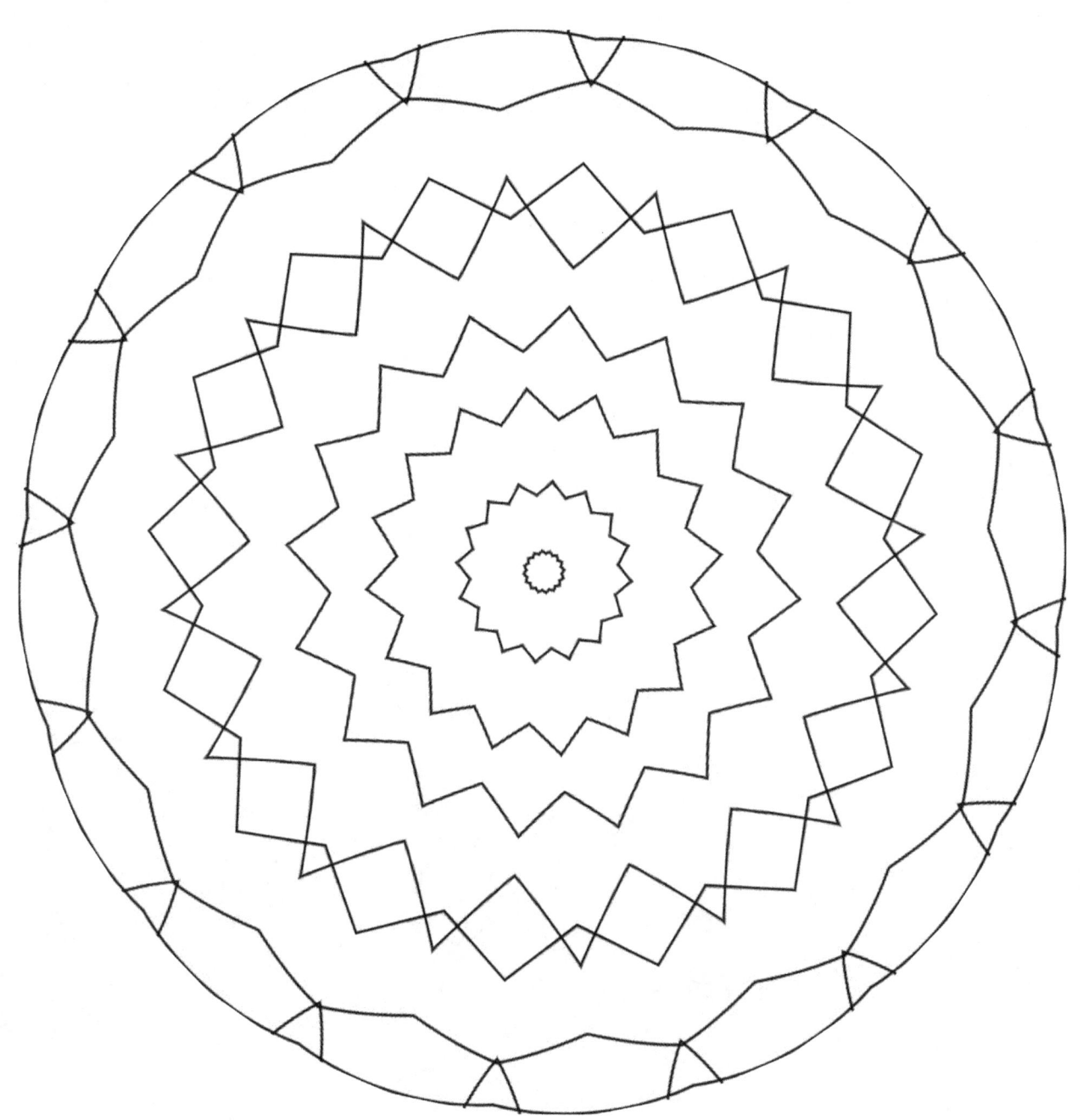

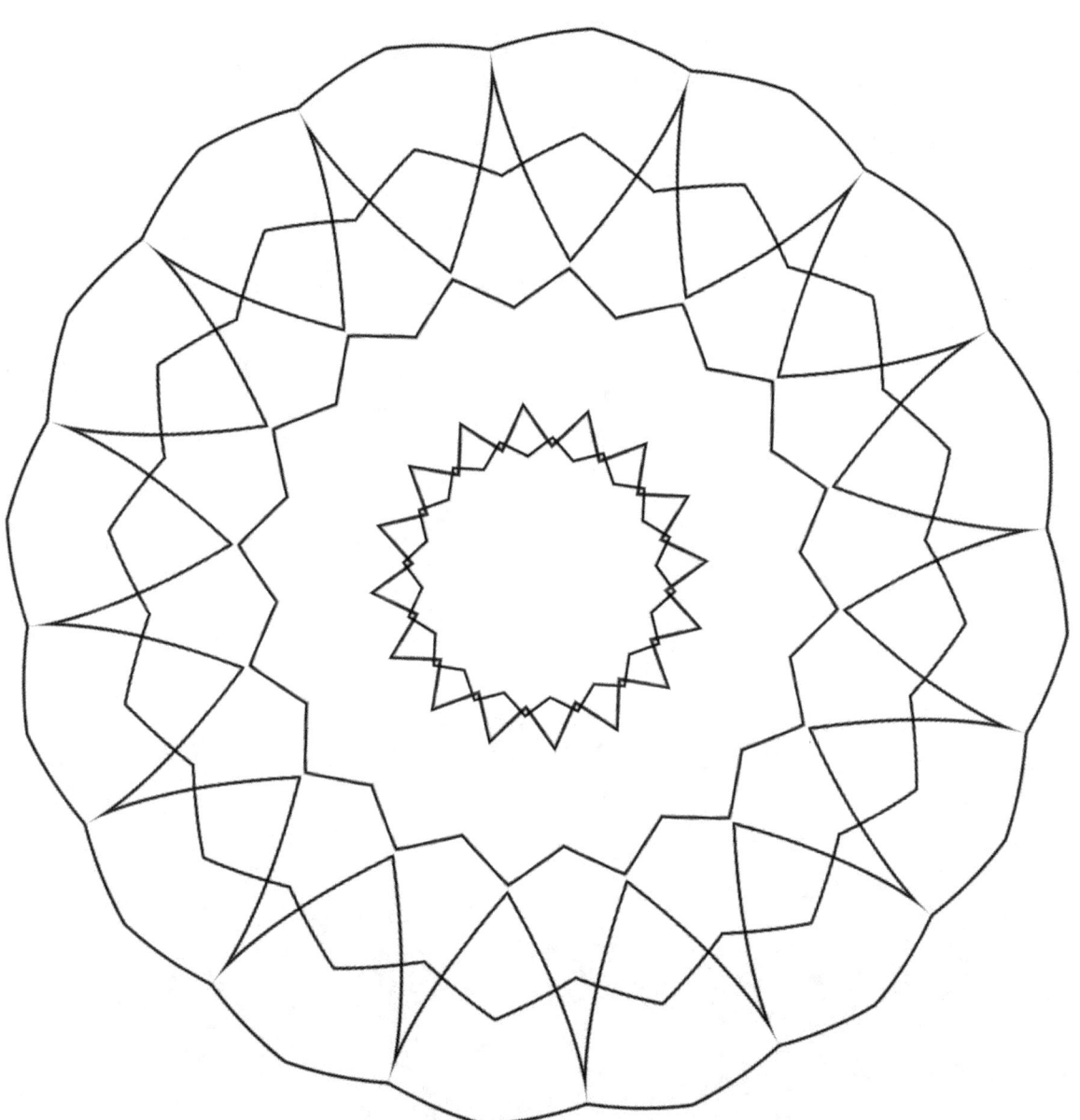

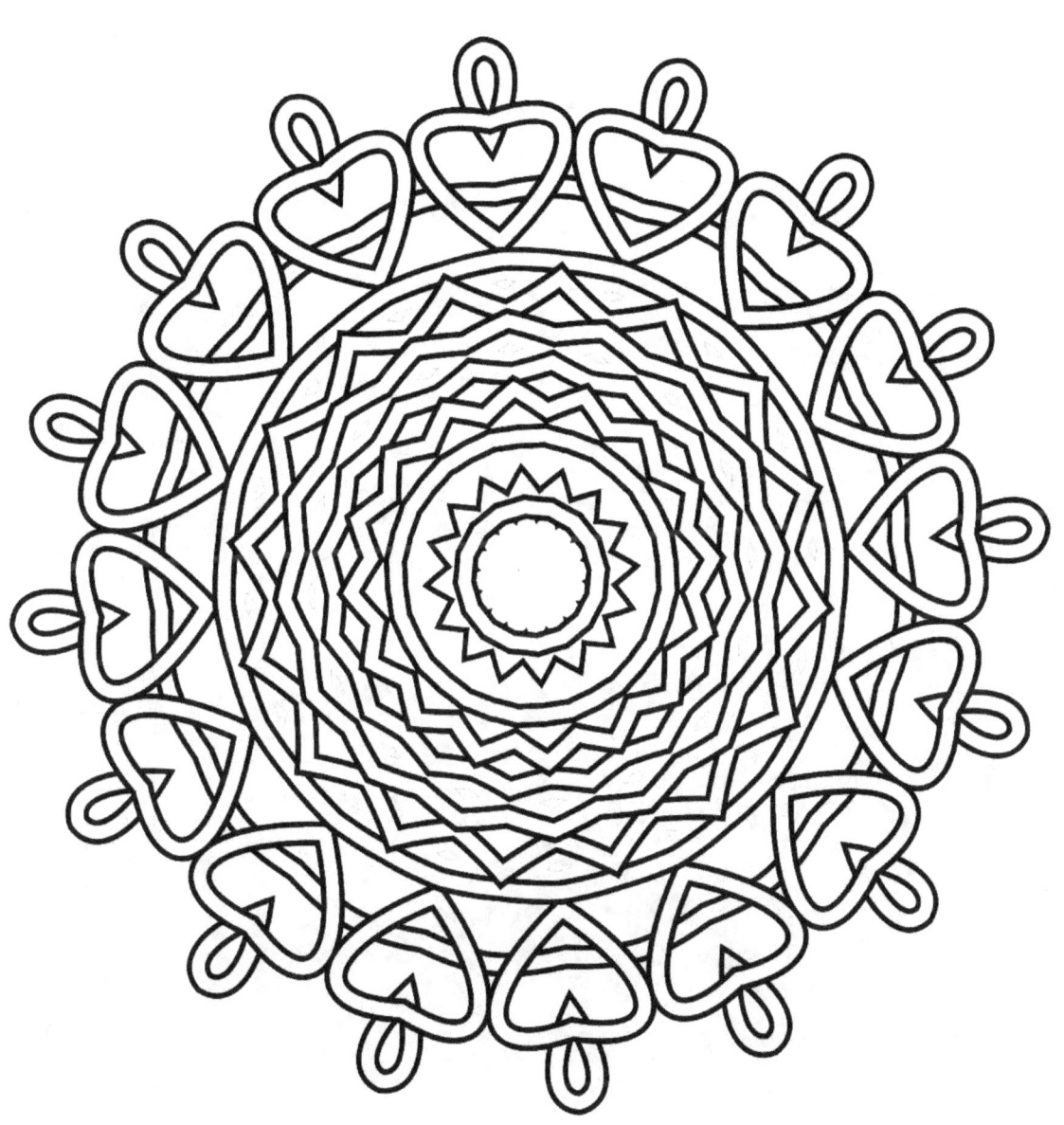

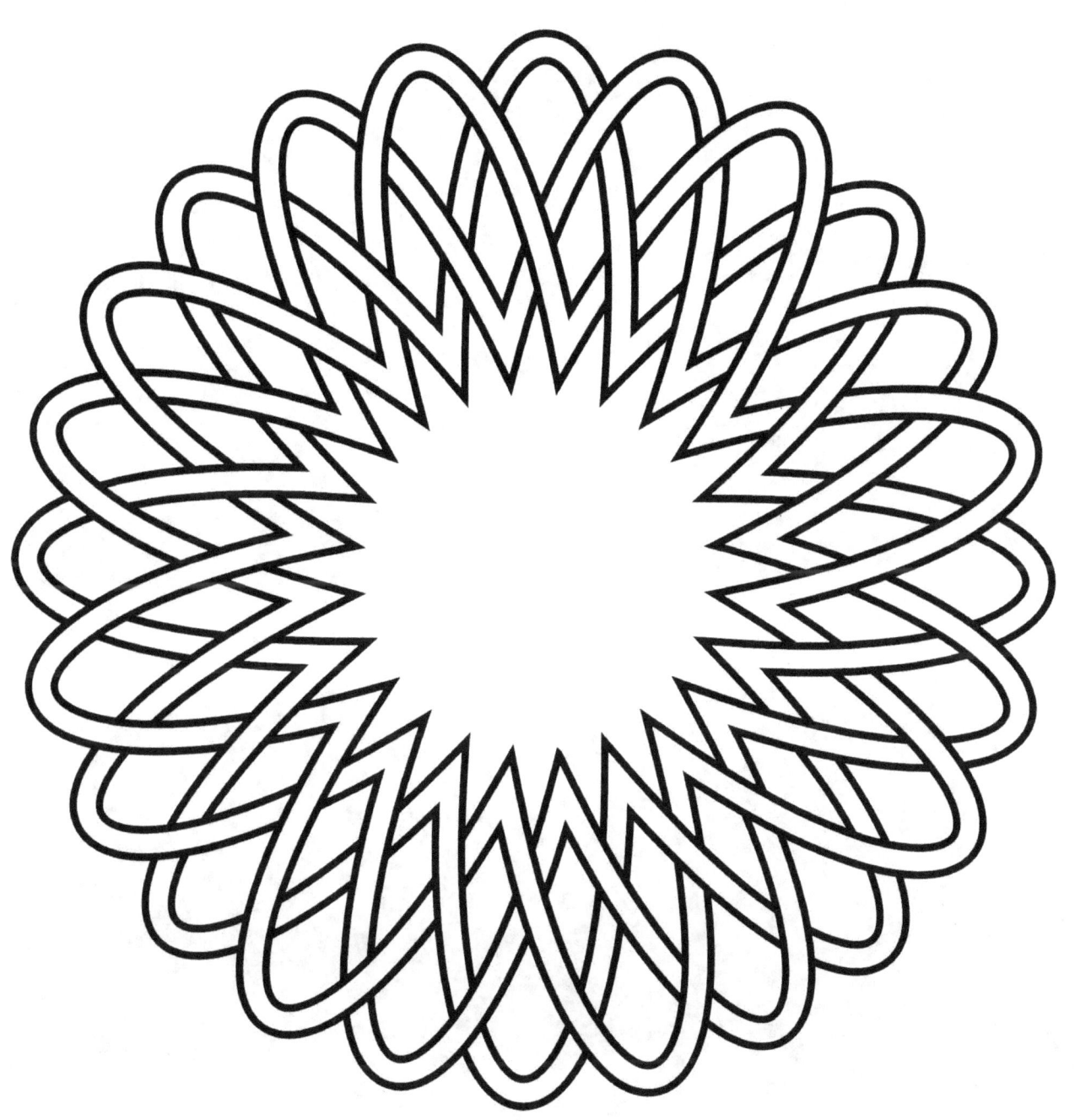

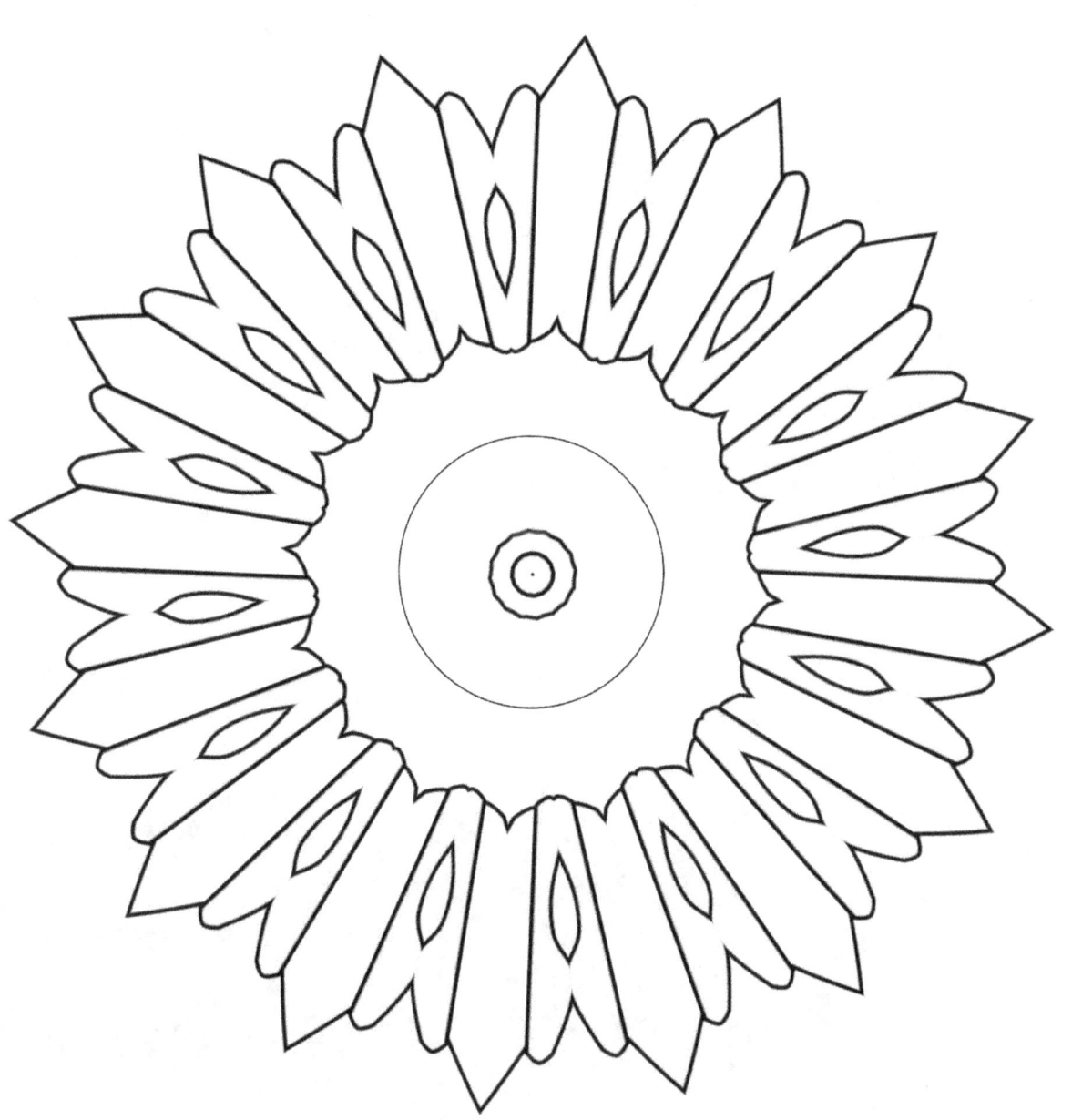

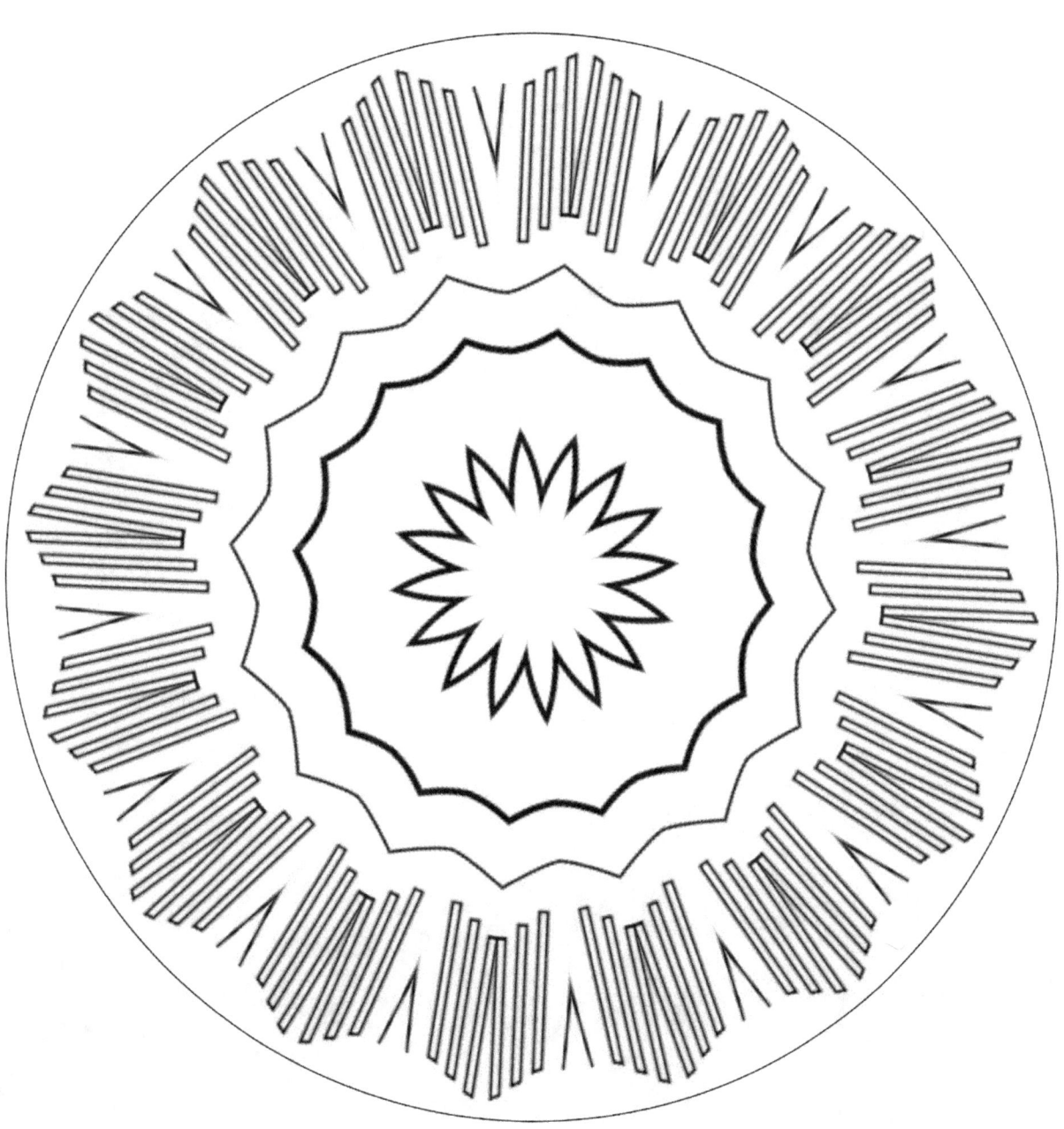

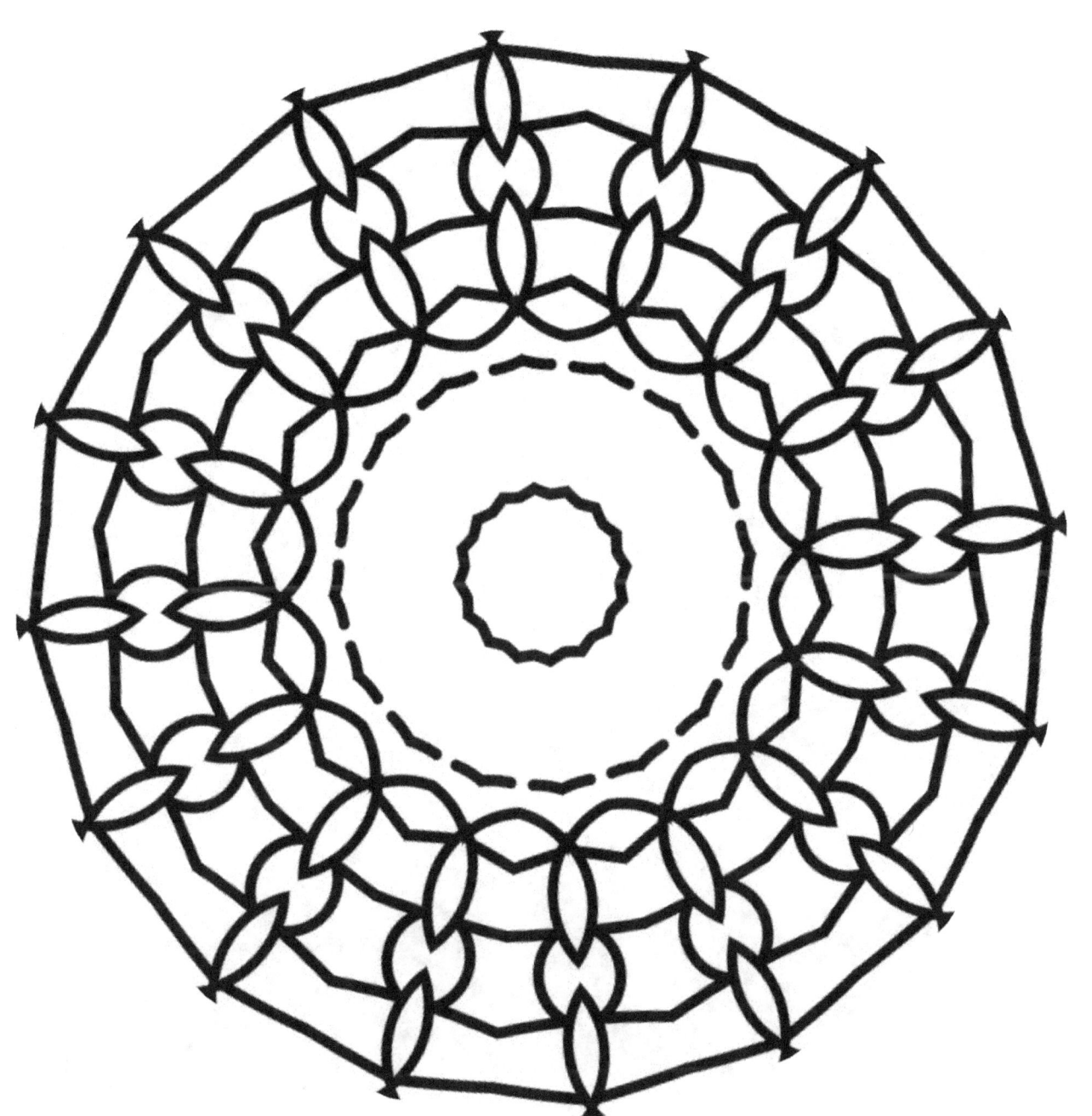

HERE IS A SECRET GIFT FOR YOU!

If you like mandalas as much as I do, you will be happy to join my secret newsletter, where you will find some good free mandalas you can download and color, plus information, techniques, videos and much much more. A place for mandala lovers!

If you decide to subscribe you will receive at most 2 emails per week, with one free design per email plus some useful information.

Go now:

http://alessandrozamboni.com/mandala

Thanks so much and see you soon!
Alessandro Zamboni

www.ingramcontent.com/pod-product-compliance
Lightning Source LLC
Chambersburg PA
CBHW080822180526
45168CB00006B/2549